Nathaniel M

Torn

Bloomsbury Methuen Drama
An imprint of Bloomsbury Publishing Plc

B L O O M S B U R Y
LONDON · OXFORD · NEW YORK · NEW DELHI · SYDNEY

Bloomsbury Methuen Drama
An imprint of Bloomsbury Publishing Plc
Imprint previously known as Methuen Drama
www.bloomsbury.com

50 Bedford Square
London
WC1B 3DP
UK

1385 Broadway
New York
NY 10018
USA

BLOOMSBURY, METHUEN DRAMA and the Diana logo
are trademarks of Bloomsbury Publishing Plc

First published 2016

© Nathaniel Martello-White 2016

Nathaniel Martello-White has asserted his rights under the Copyright, Designs
and Patents Act 1988 to be identified as the author of this work.

All rights reserved. No part of this publication may be reproduced
or transmitted in any form or by any means, electronic or mechanical,
including photocopying, recording, or any information storage or
retrieval system, without prior permission in writing from the publishers.

No responsibility for loss caused to any individual or organisation acting
on or refraining from action as a result of the material in this publication
can be accepted by Bloomsbury or the author.

All rights whatsoever in this play are strictly reserved. Requests to reproduce
the text in whole or in part should be addressed to the publisher. Application
for performance etc. by professionals or amateurs in any medium and in any
language throughout the world should be made in writing before rehearsals
begin to Judy Daish Associates Limited, 2 St Charles Place, London, W10 6EG.
No performance may be given unless a licence has been obtained and no
alteration may be made in the title or text of the play without
the author's prior written consent.

No rights in incidental music or songs contained in the Work are hereby granted
and performance rights for any performance/presentation whatsoever must be
obtained from the respective copyright owners.

British Library Cataloguing-in-Publication Data
A catalogue record for this book is available from the British Library.

ISBN: PB: 978-1-4742-9263-4
ePDF: 978-1-4742-9262-7
ePub: 978-1-4742-9264-1

Library of Congress Cataloging-in-Publication Data
A catalog record for this book is available from the Library of Congress.

Cover design: Eleanor Rose
Cover image © Vince Cavataio/Getty Images

Typeset by Country Setting, Kingsdown, Kent CT14 8ES
Printed and bound in Great Britain

THE ROYAL COURT THEATRE
PRESENTS

Torn

by Nathaniel Martello-White

Torn is part of the Royal Court's Jerwood New
Playwrights Programme, supported by the Jerwood
Charitable Foundation.

Torn was first performed at the Royal Court Jerwood Theatre Upstairs,
Sloane Square, on Wedneday 07 September 2016.

Torn

by Nathaniel Martello-White

CAST (in alphabetical order)

2nd Twin **Franc Ashman**
Aunty L **Lorna Brown**
Aunty J **Kirsty Bushell**
Brian **Roger Griffiths**
Steve **James Hillier**
Couzin **Osy Ikhile**
Angel **Adelle Leonce**
1st Twin **Indra Ové**
Brotha **Jamael Westman**

Director **Richard Twyman**
Designer **Ultz**
Lighting Designer **Charles Balfour**
Sound Designer **Gareth Fry**
Movement Director **Patricia Okenwa**
Assistant Director **Lynette Linton**
Assistant Designer **Sadeysa Greenaway–Bailey**
Casting Director **Amy Ball**
Production Manager **Marius Rønning**
Costume Supervisor **Claire Wardroper**
Dialect Coach **William Conacher**
Stage Managers **Laura Draper, Julia Slienger**
Set Construction by **Simon Black, Sam Greenfield, Nathaniel Lunn**
Scenic Artists **Grit Eckert, Megan Harrison, Faye Whiffen**

Torn
by Nathaniel Martello-White

Nathaniel Martello-White (Writer)

As Writer, theatre includes: **Blackta (Young Vic).**

As Performer, for the Royal Court: **Who Cares, Teh Internet is Serious Business, The Get Out, Gastronauts, Oxford Street.**

As Performer, other theatre includes: **People, Places & Things, Edward II (National); City Madame, A Midsummer Night's Dream, Marat/Sade (RSC); Innocence, Knives in Hens (Arcola); Joe Turner's Come & Gone (Young Vic); Bad Blood Blues (Theatre Royal, Stratford East); The Brothers Size (Actors Touring Company/Young Vic); Romeo & Juliet (National/tour).**

As Performer, television includes: **Guerilla, Silk, Death in Paradise, Misfits, Katy Brand's Big Ass Show, Law & Order: UK, Channel 4 Comedy Lab, Mongrels, Comedy Lab, Coming Up, Roman Mysteries, Doctors, Party Animals, Trial & Retribution.**

As Performer, film includes: **Hard Boiled Sweets, Life Just Is, Red Tails, The Sisterhood of the Travelling Pants 2, The Preacher, Deadmeat, Heat, Invisible.**

Franc Ashman (2nd Twin)

For the Royal Court: **Bang Bang Bang (& Out of Joint).**

Theatre includes: **The Royale, Perseverance Drive (Bush); Hopelessly Devoted (Paines Plough); This May Hurt A Bit (Out of Joint); Our Ajax (Southwark); People (National); After the Accident (Soho/The Brewery); In the Blood (Finborough); Pornography (Birmingham Rep/ Traverse/Tricycle); Cockroach (National Theatre of Scotland); Macbett, Macbeth, The Winter's Tale, Pericles (RSC).**

Television includes: **Tennison, Apple Tree Yard, Wagstaffe, DCI Banks, The Windsors, Peep Show, Birds of a Feather, Mayday, The Reckoning, Doctor Who, Law & Order: UK, Missing, Trial & Retribution, Gunrush.**

Film includes: **A Street Cat Named Bob, The Ones Below.**

Radio includes: **Behind Closed Doors: Excluded.**

Charles Balfour (Lighting Designer)

For the Royal Court: **The River (& Broadway), Choir Boy, Posh (West End), Chicken Soup With Barley, The Girlfriend Experience (& Plymouth Drum/ Young Vic), Now or Later, The Ugly One, Country Music.**

Other theatre includes: **Ma Rainey's Black Bottom (National); The Alchemist, A Midsummer Night's Dream – A Play for the Nation, Queen Anne, Hecuba, The Christmas Truce, I'll Be the Devil (RSC); Mojo, Richard III (West End); Ah Wilderness, Dirty Butterfly, The Beauty Queen of Leenane (Young Vic); The Events** (ATC/Young Vic/New York Theatre Workshop); **Minetti (Edinburgh International Festival); Guid Sisters, Mary Queen of Scots... (Royal Lyceum, Edinburgh); Jumpers for Goalposts, The Angry Brigade (Paines Plough); Orlando, The Accrington Pals (Royal Exchange, Manchester); The Hook (Northampton Royal/Liverpool Everyman); Who's Afraid of Virginia Woolf? (Crucible, Sheffield); Oh! What a Lovely War, Look Back in Anger, A Doll's House (Northern Stage); The Tempest (Liverpool Playhouse); Marilyn, Ghosts (Citizens'); The English Game, Angels in America (Headlong); The Duchess of Malfi, Hedda Gabler (West Yorkshire Playhouse); Hair, Woyzeck (Gate).**

Dance includes: **Over 30 works with the Richard Alston Dance Company (Sadler's Wells & worldwide); Hydrargyrum, Labyrinth of Love, Bloom (Rambert); Run For It (Scottish Ballet/ Cultural Olympiad); Magical Night, The Red Balloon (ROH/Aletta Collins); Woman in Memory (Tate Modern/Rosemary Butcher); Shaking World (Beijing Dance Academy); Eden/Eden (Stuttgart Ballet/San Francisco Ballet/Wayne McGregor).**

Opera/Music includes: **La Bainca Notte (Hamburg Opera); Carmen (Vlaamse Opera); OperaShots, La Voix Humaine (ROH); Carmen, Werther, Saul (Opera North); Silence Night & Dreams (Athens Acropolis); Jordan Town (Errollyn Wallen); Hagoromo, Thimble Rigging (Queen Elizabeth Hall).**

Lorna Brown (Aunty L)

For the Royal Court: **Clybourne Park, 93.2FM.**

Other theatre includes: **Oresteia (Almeida/West End); Little Light (Orange Tree); Medea, Blurred Lines, Damned by Despair, The Cry of the Cricket (National); Crowning Glory, The Big Life, Da Boyz, Funny Black Women on the Edge, Shoot to Win, One Dance Will Do (Theatre Royal, Stratford East); Fear (Bush); Short Fuses (Bristol Old Vic); Once on this Island (Hackney Empire/National Tour); Things of Dry Hours (Royal Exchange, Manchester/Gate); Trade (RSC); The Hommage Behind (West End); Mass Carib (Tour); The Weave (Soho); Anasi Steals (Talawa); Up Against the Wall (Tricycle); Othello (New Vic); Zumbi (National tour); Once on This Island (West End/ Birmingham Rep).**

Television includes: **Chewing Gum, Holby City, True Love, Outnumbered, The Catherine Tate Show, Doctors, The Bill, The Vivienne Vyle Show, The Ronnie Ancona Show, Much Ado About Nothing, French & Saunders, Family Business, Rough Treatment, Bad Girls, Casualty, Anna Lee.**

Film includes: **The Lady in the Van, Taking Stock, Les Miserables, World War Z, Gambit, Little Soldier.**

Kirsty Bushell (Aunty J)

Theatre includes: **Boys Will Be Boys (&Headlong), Disgraced, 2000 Feet Away (Bush); Hedda Gabler (Salisbury Playhouse); Antigone (Barbican); The Big Meal (Theatre Royal, Bath); Edward II, Edgar & Annabel, There is a War, 13, Danton's Death, The Voysey Inheritance, An Inspector Calls (& West End), Two Gentlemen of Verona (National); I Know How I Feel About Eve, Belongings (Hampstead); The White Devil, Twelfth Night (& Filter), The Comedy of Errors, The Tempest (RSC); Plenty, The Comedy of Errors, Girl in the Goldfish Bowl, Fen/Far Away (Crucible, Sheffield); A Thousand Stars Explode in the Sky, Angels in America, Don Juan (Lyric, Hammersmith); Peter & Vandy (503); Pornography (Birmingham Rep/Traverse/ Tricycle); Serious Money (Birmingham Rep); Blue Heart (& World tour), Testing the Echo (Out of Joint); Be My Baby (Soho); The Day That Kevin Came (Nottingham Playhouse); The Seagull (Theatre Royal, Northampton); The Importance of Being Earnest (Watermill); Antigone, Macbeth (Nuffield, Southampton).**

Television includes: **Silk, Frankie, True Love, Silent Witness, Injustice, FM, Law & Order, Pornography, Pulling, Talk to Me, Midsomer Murders, Family Man, Life Isn't All Ha Ha Hee Hee, Roger Roger, EastEnders.**

Film includes: **Really, Women & Children.**

Gareth Fry (Sound Designer)

For the Royal Court: **How To Hold Your Breath, Truth & Reconciliation, Wastwater, Chicken Soup with Barley, The City, Harvest, O Go My Man, Talking to Terrorists, Forty Winks, Night Songs, Face to the Wall, Redundant, Mountain Language, Ashes to Ashes, Under the Whaleback, The Country.**

Other theatre includes: **Harry Potter & The Cursed Child, A Christmas Carol (West End); The Encounter, The Master & Margarita, Shun-kin, Endgame (Complicité); Let The Right One In, Black Watch (National Theatre of Scotland); Boy, Game (Almeida); First Love is the Revolution (Soho); Alice in Wonderland, CBeebies Christmas Carol (CBeebies/BBC); The Glass Menagerie (Headlong); The Hudsucker Proxy (Nuffield, Southampton/Liverpool Everyman & Playhouse); John (DV8, National); Othello (Frantic Assembly); The Secret Agent (Theatre O); The Noise (Unlimited); The Cherry Orchard, Wild Swans, Hamlet (Young Vic); Othello, The Cat in the Hat, Kneehigh's A Matter Of Life & Death, Attempts on Her Life, Waves (National). The Forbidden Zone, Die Gelde Tapete, Fraulein Julie (Schaubühne, Berlin); Reise Durch die Nacht (Schauspiel, Cologne); Richard III (Old Vic/BAM/ World Tour).**

Exhibitions include: **David Bowie Is, Shakespeare: Greatest Living Playwright, Five Stages of Truth (V&A); Digital Revolution (Barbican Curve).**

Events include: **Somerset House Film4 Summer Screen & Ice Rink, Hampton Court 500 Rewind, Lighting the Sails 2014 (VIVID Live, Sydney), Soundscape Design, Opening Ceremony of the 2012 Olympic Games.**

Awards include: **Olivier Award for Best Sound Design (Waves); Helpmann Award for Best Sound Design, Olivier Award for Best Sound Design (Black Watch); IRNE Award (Wild Swans).**

Sadeysa Greenaway-Bailey (Assistant Designer)

As Assistant Designer, for the Royal Court: **The River, Choir Boy, The Westbridge.**

As Assistant Designer, other theatre includes: **I Capuleti e i Montecchi (Landes Theater Niederbayern, Germany); La Musica, The Changeling (Young Vic).**

As Associate Designer, other theatre includes: **Ma Rainey's Black Bottom (National); Kingston 14 (Theatre Royal, Stratford East); The Epic Adventure of Nhamo the Manyika Warrior & His Sexy Wife Chipo (Tricycle/Tiata Fahodzi).**

As Designer, theatre includes: **Orphans of the Grange, Gargantua, The Endless Night (Tricycle); The Far Side (South Hill Park); The Legend Of Hamba (Tiata Fahodzi).**

As Scenic Artist & Costume Prop Maker, work includes: **Beauty & The Beast (Theatre Royal, Stratford East); European Games Opening Ceremony 2015, Azerbaijan; Carnival Messiah (Harewood House & Mahogany Carnival Arts Ltd).**

Sadeysa Greenaway-Bailey is a Designer and Scenic Artist. She trained at Rose Bruford College.

Roger Griffiths (Brian)

Theatre includes: **All My Sons (Royal Exchange, Manchester); One Monkey Don't Stop No Show (Tricycle); The Graft (Theatre Royal, Stratford East); Macbeth, Black Poppies (National); Job Rocking, O Babylon! (Riverside Studios).**

Television includes: **Death in Paradise, Vexed, Doctors, Casualty, Rock & Chips, Hustle, Doctor Who, Holby City, Dubplate Drama, My Family, EastEnders, French & Saunders, Family Affairs, Paradise Heights, Dr. Terrible's House of Horrible, Heartbeat, Casualty, Lenny Henry in Pieces, A Brand Spanking New Show, Trust, The Bill, Comin' Acha!, Forgive & Forget, Mike & Angelo, Chef, Thief Takers, Ruth Rendell, Desmond's.**

Film includes: **Hard Time Bus, Communion, Dead Meat, Batman Begins, Buffalo Soldiers.**

James Hillier (Steve)

Theatre includes: **The Deep Blue Sea (Watermill); Venice Preserv'd (The Spectator's Guild); Pick One, Church... (Theatre Uncut for The Young/UK); I'm With The Band (Traverse/UK Tour); Casablanca (Future Cinema); Sluts Of Sutton Drive, Blue Surge, Something Cloudy Something Clear (Finborough); Titanic (MAC); 66 Books (Bush); The Water Engine (Old Vic); Clockwork Orange (Citizens); Closer (Theatre Royal, Northampton); Through The Glass (National); The Recruiting Officer (Litchfield); The Homecoming (Royal Exchange, Manchester); Lulu (Almeida); Journey's End (Drill Hall); Trips**

(Birmingham Rep); Le Bourgeois Gentlehomme (Upstairs at The Gatehouse).

Television includes: **The Crown, Tennison, Frontier, Casualty, Survivors, Holby Blue, EastEnders, Goldplated, Blackbeard, Lucy Sullivan Is Getting Married, The Bill, The Rise & Fall of Rome: Revolution, Holby City, Silent Witness, The Inspector Lynley Mysteries, Running Time, All The King's Men, Great Expectations, An Unsuitable Job For A Woman.**

Film includes: **The Brother, My Horrible Love, Mr Invisible, Fired, Stagknight, Tomorrow's Forecast, Mr Mzuza, The British, London's Burning, The King's Head, Locock, Simon's Making A Film, Sex & Lies, Four Feathers, Long Time Dead.**

James is Artistic Director for Defibrillator Theatre Company with directing credits including **Insignificance** by Terry Johnson (New York), **The Armour** by Ben Ellis, **The Hotel Plays** by Tennessee Williams and **Hard Feelings** by Doug Lucie.

Osy Ikhile (Couzin)

Theatre includes: **Sweet Love Remembered** (Globe); **Your Number's Up** (Roundhouse).

Television includes: **Childhood's End, The Fear, Fresh Meat, Twenty Twelve, Blackout, Tom & Jenny, Misfits, Phone Shop.**

Film includes: **Daphne, Sand Castle, Beautiful Devils, Tarzan, Mission: Impossible – Rogue Nation, Kill Your Friends, Jet Trash, In the Heart of the Sea, Victim, The Anomaly.**

Adelle Leonce (Angel)

Theatre includes: **In the Night Time** (Gate); **Light Shining in Buckinghamshire** (National); **Tipping the Velvet, A Streetcar Named Desire, Woyzeck, Chamber Piece, Glitterland, A Series of Increasingly Impossible Acts** (& Tricycle), **A Stab in the Dark** (Lyric, Hammersmith).

Television includes: **Ordinary Lies, DCI Banks, Shameless, Vera, In the Garden.**

Lynette Linton (Assistant Director)

As Assistant Director, for the Royal Court: **A View from the Moon** (& Birmingham Rep) Live Lunch.

As Assistant Director, other theatre includes: **Gutted** (Theatre Royal, Stratford East); **Image of An Unknown Young Woman, The Christians** (Gate).

As Director, theatre includes: **Indenture** (Dark Horse Festival); **Assata: She Who Struggles** (Young Vic); **Naked** (Vault Festival); **Pornado** (Theatre Royal Stratford, East); **This Wide Night** (Albany).

As Co-Director, theatre includes: **Chicken Palace** (Theatre Royal, Stratford East).

As Writer, theatre includes: **Step** (& school tour), **Chicken Palace** (Theatre Royal, Stratford East); **Ergo Sum** (Theatre Deli).

Lynette Linton is a director and playwright she trained on the StoneCrabs Young Directors Course where she was also awarded the Jack Petchy award. Her new play Hashtag Lightie is

in development with Team Angelica. She is the current Associate Director of the Gate Theatre.

Patricia Okenwa (Movement Director)

As Choreographer, theatre includes: **Collapse, Nest, Casting Traces** (NMC); **Hydrargyrum** (Rambert Repertoire/Tour); **Station to Station** (Barbican/NMC); **Il Void** (Ignition Dance Festival); **No. 1 Convergence, Three Pieces, Solo, Longing, Veridita, Hold Me, Mammon, Sleevless Scerzo, Idelu** (Rambert/Queen Elisabeth Hall/Lilian Baylis Sadler's Wells/Linbury ROH2/ The Place) **Collapse** (New Movement Collective/Southbank Centre); **Nightflowers** (Robin Howard); **Foolish Giggles Sudden Tears** (Resolution! The Place/ Work 1 Festival, Valencia).

As Performer, theatre includes: **Transfigured Night, Frames, Four Elements, Rooster, The Castaways, Subterrain, Labyrinth of Love, L' Après Midi d'un Faune, Dark Arteries, What Wild Ecstasy, Comedy of Change, Eternal Light, Lady into Fox, Constant Speed, Sounddance, Rainforest, Pond Way, Infinity, Swamp, Dark Elegies, Steel Garden, Hush, Gran Partita, Tragedy of Fashion** (Rambert).

Patricia has worked as a dancer for New Movement Collective in collaboration with AAIS since 2011 with performances in Covent Garden, Madrid, Architecture Association London and Cologne. She was part of the Ensemblegroup in 2004, taking part in the Hip Dance Festival in 2003 and the Embodying Ambiguites Project by Emilyn Claid.

Indra Ové (1st Twin)

Theatre includes: **The Curious Incident of the Dog in the Night-Time, The Seagull, Blinded by the Sun, A Midsummer Night's Dream** (National); **Twelve Women** (Ovalhouse); **Yes Prime Minister** (West End/Tour); **Twelve Angry Women** (Gutted/Lion & Unicorn); **Etta Jenks** (Finborough); **Under One Roof** (Kings, Glasgow/V&A); **Peer Gynt** (Arcola); **900 Oneota** (Lyric, Hammersmith); **Timon of Athens** (Young Vic).

Television includes: **Holby City, Glue, Dumping Ground, Topsy & Tim, Casualty, Doctors, Midsomer Murders, Best Man, The New Worst Witch, Attachments, Bugs, Space Island One, She's Out.**

Film includes: **Jurassic, Second Spring, Dubois, Still, Wonder, Mr Invisible, Hellhounds, My One & Only, Blinding Lights, Cold Dead Hands, Other, Club Le Monde, It's All About Love, Resident Evil, The Dreamer, Cleopatra, More is Less, The Fifth Element, Othello, Interview With a Vampire.**

Radio includes: **Community Flock, Madame Butterfly, The Wide Sargasso, The Audition.**

Richard Twyman (Director)

For the Royal Court: **Told From The Inside – Goats & The Final Return, You For Me For You, Fireworks, The Djinns of Eidgah, Phil in Space, PIIGS, A New Song.**

Other theatre includes: **Harrogate** (HighTide); **Henry**

IV Pt II (RSC); Ditch (Old Vic Tunnels/HighTide); 66 Books (Bush); Give Me Your Hand (Irish Rep, New York).

Richard is Artistic Director of English Touring Theatre. He was previously Associate Director (International) at the Royal Court.

Ultz (Designer)

For the Royal Court: **Jerusalem (& Broadway), The River (& Broadway), Mojo (& West End), Choir Boy, Wig Out!, The Westbridge, Chicken Soup with Barley, Off the Endz, The Family Plays, The Winterling, Stoning Mary, A Girl in a Car with a Man, Fresh Kills, The Weather/Bear Hug, Bone, Fallout, The Night Heron, Fireface, Lift Off.**

Other theatre includes: **Ma Rainey's Black Bottom, Blood & Gifts, The Ramayana (National); La Musica, The Changeling, The Beauty Queen of Leenane (Young Vic); Kingston 14 (Theatre Royal, Stratford East); The Harder They Come (Theatre Royal, Stratford East/Barbican/West End); Iya-Ile, The Estate, The Gods Are Not To Blame (Tiata Fahodzi at Arcola/Soho); Boy (Costumes only – Almeida).**

Opera includes: **Gloriana (ROH); Lohengrin (Bavarian State Opera); Ariodante (Aix-en-Provence Festival/Dutch National Opera); Macbeth, Falstaff (Glyndebourne Festival); Cavalleria Rusticana/I Pagliacci, The Bitter Tears of Petra von Kant, Powder Her Face (ENO).**

Awards include: **Olivier Award for Best Set Design (Jerusalem); Olivier Award for Outstanding Achievement in an Affiliate Theatre (Pied Piper); Off West End Award for Best Set Design (The Beauty Queen of Leenane).**

As an Associate Artist at Stratford East, Ultz develops and directs new pieces of Urban Music Theatre. These have included Da Boyz, Pied Piper – a Hip Hop Dance Revolution (created with Boy Blue Entertainment) and Jean Genet's play The Blacks Remixed (co-directed).

Jamael Westman (Brotha)

Theatre includes: **Bricks & Pieces (Tiata Fahodzi); Take a Deep Breath & Breathe (CLF Art Cafe); Stop Kiss (Leicester Square); Othello (Brockley Jack); Romeo & Juliet (Ovalhouse); Our Boys (South London Theatre).**

Television includes: **Casualty.**

Film includes: **Kebab, Identicals.**

JERWOOD CHARITABLE FOUNDATION

Jerwood New Playwrights is a longstanding partnership between Jerwood Charitable Foundation and the Royal Court. Each year, Jerwood New Playwrights supports the production of three new works by emerging writers, all of whom are in the first 10 years of their career.

The Royal Court carefully identifies playwrights whose careers would benefit from the challenge and profile of being fully produced either in the Jerwood Downstairs or Jerwood Upstairs Theatres at the Royal Court.

Since 1994, the programme has produced a collection of challenging and outspoken works which explore a variety of new forms and voices and so far has supported the production of 83 new plays. These plays include: Joe Penhall's **Some Voices**, Nick Grosso's **Peaches** and **Real Classy Affair**, Judy Upton's **Ashes and Sand**, Sarah Kane's **Blasted, Cleansed** and **4.48 Psychosis**, Michael Wynne's **The Knocky** and **The People are Friendly**, Judith Johnson's **Uganda**, Sebastian Barry' s **The Steward of Christendom**, Jez Butterworth's **Mojo**, Mark Ravenhill's **Shopping and Fucking**, Ayub Khan Din's **East is East** and **Notes on Falling Leaves**, Martin McDonagh's **The Beauty Queen of Leenane**, Jess Walters' **Cockroach, Who?**, Tamantha Hammerschlag's **Backpay**, Connor McPherson's **The Weir**, Meredith Oakes' **Faith**, Rebecca Prichard's **Fair Game**, Roy Williams' **Lift Off, Clubland** and **Fallout**, Richard Bean's **Toast** and **Under the Whaleback**, Gary Mitchell's **Trust** and **The Force of Change**, Mick Mahoney's **Sacred Heart** and **Food Chain**, Marina Carr's **On Raftery's Hill**, David Eldridge's **Under the Blue Sky** and **Incomplete and Random Acts of Kindness**, David Harrower's **Presence**, Simon Stephens' **Herons, Country Music**

and **Motortown**, Leo Butler's **Redundant** and **Lucky Dog**, Enda Walsh's **Bedbound**, David Greig's **Outlying Islands**, Zinnie Harris' **Nightingale and Chase**, Grae Cleugh's **Fucking Games**, Rona Munro's **Iron**, Ché Walker's **Fleshwound**, Laura Wade's **Breathing Corpses**, debbie tucker green's **Stoning Mary**, Gregory Burke's **On Tour**, Stella Feehily's **O Go My Man**, Simon Farquhar's **Rainbow Kiss**, April de Angelis, Stella Feehily, Tanika Gupta, Chloe Moss and Laura Wade's **Catch**, Polly Stenham's **That Face** and **Tusk Tusk**, Mike Bartlett's **My Child**, Fiona Evans' **Scarborough**, Levi David Addai's **Oxford Street**, Bola Agbaje's **Gone Too Far!** and **Off The Endz**, Alexi Kaye Campbell's **The Pride**, Alia Bano's **Shades**, Tim Crouch's **The Author**, DC Moore's **The Empire**, Anya Reiss' **Spur of the Moment** and **The Acid Test**, Penelope Skinner's **The Village Bike**, Rachel De-lahay's **The Westbridge** and **Routes**, Nick Payne's **Constellations**, Vivienne Franzmann's **The Witness** and **Pests**, E. V. Crowe's **Hero**, Anders Lustgarten's **If You Don't Let Us Dream, We Won't Let You Sleep**, Suhayla El-Bushra's **Pigeons**, Clare Lizzimore's **Mint**, Alistair McDowall's **Talk Show**, Rory Mullarkey's **The Wolf From The Door**, Molly Davies' **God Bless The Child**, Diana Nneka Atuona's **Liberian Girl**, Cordelia Lynn's **Lela & Co.**, Nicola Wilson's **Plaques & Tangles**, Stef Smith's **Human Animals** and Charlene James' **Cuttin' It**.

Jerwood Charitable Foundation is dedicated to imaginative and responsible revenue funding of the arts, supporting artists to develop and grow at important stages in their careers. It works with artists across art forms, from dance and theatre to literature, music and the visual arts.

jerwoodcharitablefoundation.org

THE ROYAL COURT THEATRE

The Royal Court Theatre is the writers' theatre. It is the leading force in world theatre for energetically cultivating writers – undiscovered, emerging and established.

Through the writers, the Royal Court is at the forefront of creating restless, alert, provocative theatre about now. We open our doors to the unheard voices and free thinkers that, through their writing, change our way of seeing.

Over 120,000 people visit the Royal Court in Sloane Square, London, each year and many thousands more see our work elsewhere through transfers to the West End and New York, UK and international tours, digital platforms, our residencies across London, and our site-specific work. Through all our work we strive to inspire audiences and influence future writers with radical thinking and provocative discussion.

The Royal Court's extensive development activity encompasses a diverse range of writers and artists and includes an ongoing programme of writers' attachments, readings, workshops and playwriting groups. Twenty years of the International Department's pioneering work around the world means the Royal Court has relationships with writers on every continent.

Within the past sixty years, John Osborne, Samuel Beckett, Arnold Wesker, Ann Jellicoe, Howard Brenton and David Hare have started their careers at the Court.

Many others including Caryl Churchill, Athol Fugard, Mark Ravenhill, Simon Stephens, debbie tucker green, Sarah Kane - and, more recently, Lucy Kirkwood, Nick Payne, Penelope Skinner and Alistair McDowall - have followed.

The Royal Court has produced many iconic plays from Laura Wade's **Posh** to Jez Butterworth's **Jerusalem** and Martin McDonagh's **Hangmen**.

Royal Court plays from every decade are now performed on stage and taught in classrooms and universities across the globe.

It is because of this commitment to the writer that we believe there is no more important theatre in the world than the Royal Court.

Supported using public funding by
ARTS COUNCIL ENGLAND

ROYAL

COMING UP AT THE ROYAL COURT

JERWOOD THEATRE DOWNSTAIRS

15 Sep - 22 Oct
Father Comes Home From The Wars
(Parts 1, 2 & 3)
by Suzan-Lori Parks

17 Nov - 14 Jan
The Children
by Lucy Kirkwood

25 Jan - 11 Feb
Escaped Alone
by Caryl Churchill

JERWOOD THEATRE UPSTAIRS

20 - 29 Oct
The Royal Court Theatre, house, and HighTide
present The HighTide Production
Harrogate
by Al Smith

10 Nov - 22 Dec
The Sewing Group
by E V Crowe

10 Jan - 11 Feb
Royal Court Theatre and Royal Exchange Theatre
WISH LIST
by Katherine Soper

royalcourttheatre.com

Supported using public funding by
**ARTS COUNCIL
ENGLAND**

Sloane Square London, SW1W 8AS
🐦 royalcourt 📘 royalcourttheatre
🚇 Sloane Square ⇌ Victoria Station

ROYAL COURT SUPPORTERS

The Royal Court is a registered charity and not-for-profit company. We need to raise £1.7 million every year in addition to our core grant from the Arts Council and our ticket income to achieve what we do.

We have significant and longstanding relationships with many generous organisations and individuals who provide vital support. Royal Court supporters enable us to remain the writers' theatre, find stories from everywhere and create theatre for everyone.

We can't do it without you.

The Genesis Foundation supports the Royal Court's work with International Playwrights. Bloomberg supports Beyond the Court. Jerwood Charitable Foundation supports emerging writers through the Jerwood New Playwrights series. The Pinter Commission is given annually by his widow, Lady Antonia Fraser, to support a new commission at the Royal Court.

PUBLIC FUNDING

Arts Council England, London
British Council

CHARITABLE DONATIONS

The Bryan Adams Charitable Trust
The Austin & Hope Pilkington Trust
Martin Bowley Charitable Trust
Gerald Chapman Fund
CHK Charities
The City Bridge Trust
The Clifford Chance Foundation
Cockayne - Grants for the Arts
The Ernest Cook Trust
Cowley Charitable Trust
The Dorset Foundation
The Eranda Foundation
Lady Antonia Fraser for The Pinter Commission

Genesis Foundation
The Golden Bottle Trust
The Haberdashers' Company
The Paul Hamlyn Foundation
Roderick & Elizabeth Jack
Jerwood Charitable Foundation
Kirsh Foundation
The Mackintosh Foundation
Marina Kleinwort Trust
The Andrew Lloyd Webber Foundation
The London Community Foundation
John Lyon's Charity
Clare McIntyre's Bursary
The Andrew W. Mellon Foundation
The Mercers' Company
The Portrack Charitable Trust
The David & Elaine Potter Foundation
The Richard Radcliffe Charitable Trust
Rose Foundation
Royal Victoria Hall Foundation
The Sackler Trust
The Sobell Foundation
John Thaw Foundation
The Vandervell Foundation
Sir Siegmund Warburg's Voluntary Settlement
The Garfield Weston Foundation
The Wolfson Foundation

CORPORATE SPONSORS

AKA
AlixPartners
Aqua Financial Solutions Ltd
Bloomberg
Colbert
Edwardian Hotels, London

Fever-Tree
Gedye & Sons
Kirkland & Ellis International LLP
Kudos
MAC
Nyetimber

BUSINESS MEMBERS

Auerbach & Steele Opticians
CNC – Communications & Network Consulting
Cream
Hugo Boss UK
Lansons
Left Bank Pictures
Rockspring Property Investment Managers
Tetragon Financial Group
Vanity Fair

DEVELOPMENT COUNCIL

Majella Altschuler
Piers Butler
Sarah Chappatte
Cas Donald
Celeste Fenichel
Piers Gibson
Emma Marsh
Angelie Moledina
Anatol Orient
Andrew Rodger
Deborah Shaw
Sian Westerman

INDIVIDUAL SUPPORTERS

Artistic Director's Circle
Eric Abraham
Cas Donald
Lydia & Manfred Gorvy
Jack & Linda Keenan
Mandeep Manku
Miles Morland
Anatol Orient
NoraLee & Jon Sedmak
Deborah Shaw &
Stephen Marquardt
Angelie & Shafin Moledina
Jan & Michael Topham
Mahdi Yahya

Writers' Circle
Jordan Cook
Mark & Charlotte Cunningham
Jane Featherstone
Piers & Melanie Gibson
Luke Johnson
Duncan Matthews QC
Ian & Carol Sellars
Matthew & Sian Westerman
The Wilhelm Helmut Trust
Anonymous

Directors' Circle
Dr Kate Best
Katie Bradford
Chris & Alison Cabot
Louis Greig
David Harding
Roderick & Elizabeth Jack
Melanie J Johnson
Nicola Kerr
Philip & Joan Kingsley
Emma Marsh
Rachel Mason
Andrew & Ariana Rodger
Anonymous (2)

Platinum Members
Moira Andreae
Nick Archdale
Michael Bennett
Clive & Helena Butler
Piers Butler
Gavin & Lesley Casey
Sarah & Philippe Chappatte
Michael & Arlene Cohrs
Clyde Cooper

Mr & Mrs Cross
Andrew & Amanda Cryer
Alison Davies
Matthew Dean
Sarah Denning
Denise & Randolph Dumas
Robyn Durie
Mark & Sarah Evans
Sally & Giles Everist
Celeste & Peter Fenichel
Emily Fletcher
The Edwin Fox Foundation
Dominic & Claire Freemantle
Beverley Gee
Nick & Julie Gould
The Richard Grand Foundation
Jill Hackel & Andrzej Zarzycki
Carol Hall
Peter & Debbie Hargreaves
Sam & Caroline Haubold
David & Sheila Hodgkinson
Mr & Mrs Gordon Holmes
Damien Hyland
Amanda & Chris Jennings
Susanne Kapoor
David P Kaskel
 & Christopher A Teano
Vincent & Amanda Keaveny
Peter & Maria Kellner
Mr & Mrs Pawel Kisielewski
Daisy & Richard Littler
Rosemary Leith
Kathryn Ludlow
Dr Ekaterina Malievskaia
 & George Goldsmith
Christopher Marek Rencki
Mrs Janet Martin
Andrew McIver
David & Elizabeth Miles
Barbara Minto
Siobhan Murphy
M. Murphy Altschuler
Peter & Maggie Murray-Smith
Ann & Gavin Neath CBE
Emma O'Donoghue
Kate O'Neill
Adam Oliver-Watkins
Crispin Osborne
Andrea & Hilary Ponti
Greg & Karen Reid
Paul & Gill Robinson
Sir Paul & Lady Ruddock
William & Hilary Russell
Sally & Anthony Salz
João Saraiva e Silva
Anita Scott

Jenny Shann
Bhags Sharma
Dr. Wendy Sigle
Andy Simpkin
Brian Smith
Mr John Soler
Jessica Speare-Cole
Maria Sukkar
Mrs Caroline Thomas
The Ulrich Family
Monica B Voldstad
Anne-Marie Williams
Sir Robert & Lady Wilson
Kate & Michael Yates
Anonymous (6)

With thanks to our Friends, Silver and Gold members whose support we greatly appreciate.

Innovation partner

 Supported using public funding by
ARTS COUNCIL ENGLAND

Royal Court Theatre
Sloane Square,
London SW1W 8AS
Tel: 020 7565 5050
info@royalcourttheatre.com
www.royalcourttheatre.com

Artistic Director
Vicky Featherstone
Executive Producer
Lucy Davies

Associate Directors
Lucy Morrison, Hamish Pirie, John Tiffany, Graham Whybrow
Associate Designer
Chloe Lamford
Associate Playwright
Simon Stephens
Artistic Associates
Ola Animashawun, Chris Sonnex*
Trainee Director
Grace Gummer‡

International Director
Elyse Dodgson
Associate Director (International)
Sam Pritchard
International Assistant
Sarah Murray

General Manager
Catherine Thornborrow
Assistant Producer
Minna Sharpe
Projects Producer
Chris James
Assistant to the Executive
Ryan Govin
Trainee Administrator (Producing)
Jerome Mitchell§
Trainee Administrator (Projects & Literary)
Zahra Beswick§

Deputy Head of Young Court
Romana Flello
Young Court Assistant
Maia Clarke

Literary Manager
Chris Campbell
Deputy Literary Manager
Louise Stephens
Literary Assistant
Adam Narat

Head of Casting
Amy Ball
Casting Assistant
Arthur Carrington

Head of Production
Matt Noddings
Production Manager
Marius Rønning
Head of Lighting
Jack Williams
Lighting Deputy
Steven Binks
Lighting Technicians
Jess Faulks, Matthew Harding
JTD Programmer & Operator
Catriona Carter
Head of Stage
Steven Stickler
Stage Deputy
Dan Lockett
Stage Chargehand
Lee Crimmen
Chargehand & Building Maintenance Technician
Matt Livesey
Head of Sound
David McSeveney
Sound Deputy
Emily Legg
Head of Costume
Lucy Walshaw
Wardrobe Manager
Gina Lee
Costume Apprentice
Courtney Musselwhite
Company Manager
Joni Carter

Finance Director
Helen Perryer
Financial Controller
Ed Hales
Financial Administrator
Rosie Mortimer
Accounts Assistant
Sian Ruffles
Finance Trainee
Kadisha Williams§

Head of Press & Publicity
Anoushka Hay
Communications Trainee (Press)
Daniela Lewy§

Head of Marketing
Holly Conneely
Marketing Manager
Dion Wilson
Marketing Officer
Alex Green
Communications Trainee (Marketing)
Audrey Aidoo–Davies§

Head of Sales
Liam Geoghegan
Box Office Manager
Helen Corbett
Box Office Sales Assistants
Will Bourdillon*, Laura Duncanson, Joe Hodgson, Margaret Perry*

Development Director
Rebecca Kendall
Deputy Development Director (Maternity Leave)
Lucy Buxton
Deputy Development Director (Maternity Cover)
Liv Nilssen
Development Manager (Maternity Leave)
Luciana Lawlor
Corporate & Events Manager
Nadia Vistisen
Development Officer
Camilla Start
Head of Trusts
Fran Pilcher
Development Officer
Charlotte Cole

Theatre Manager (maternity leave)
Rachel Dudley
Theatre Manager (maternity cover)
Louise Glover
Front of House Manager
Adam Lawler
Duty House Managers
Flo Bourne, Elinor Keber, Tanya Shields
Cover Duty House Managers
Rhiannon Handy, Tristan Rogers
Caretaker
Christian Rudolph
Bar & Kitchen Manager
Ali Christian
Deputy Bar & Kitchen Manager
Robert Smael
Assistant Bar & Kitchen Manager
Jared Thomas
Head Chef
Francesco Ripanti
Bookshop Manager
Simon David
Bookshop Assistant
Eleanor Crosswell*

Stage Door/Reception
Paul Lovegrove, Tiiu Mortley, Jane Wainwright

Thanks to all of our Ushers and Bar & Kitchen staff.

§
Posts supported by
The Sackler Trust
Trainee Scheme

‡
The post of Trainee Director is supported by an anonymous donor.

* Part-time.

ENGLISH STAGE COMPANY

President
Dame Joan Plowright CBE

Honorary Council
Sir Richard Eyre CBE
Alan Grieve CBE
Phyllida Lloyd CBE
Martin Paisner CBE

Council Chairman
Anthony Burton CBE
Vice Chairman
Graham Devlin CBE
Members
Jennette Arnold OBE
Judy Daish
Sir David Green KCMG
Joyce Hytner OBE
Stephen Jeffreys
Emma Marsh
Roger Michell
James Midgley
Anita Scott
Lord Stewart Wood

The Royal Court works with a huge variety of companies ranging from small local businesses to large global firms. The Court has been at the cutting edge of new drama for more than 50 years and, situated in the heart of Chelsea, makes the perfect evening for a night of unique client entertaining.

By becoming a Business Member, your company will be given an allocation of London's hottest tickets with the chance of booking in for sold out shows, the opportunity to entertain your clients in our stunning Balcony Bar and exclusive access to the creative members of staff and cast members.

BECOME A BUSINESS MEMBER

To discuss Business Membership at the Royal Court, please contact:
Nadia Vistisen, Corporate & Events Manager
nadiavistisen@royalcourttheatre.com
020 7565 5030

The English Stage Company at the Royal Court Theatre is a registered charity (No. 231242).

Torn

To Gemma and Jerome

Author's Notes

A bare stage scattered with chairs around it. Angel enters and with serious intent sets the chairs in a circle. She exits and then re-enters with a plastic jug of water and cups, and sets a tea area, north of the circle, which operates as a time-out area.

The Brooks family enter one by one, and congregate by the entrance awkwardly, where they write their names with black felt tip on white stickers, which they apply to themselves and then gradually take their seats within the circle.

They have been gathered by Angel who observes them as they enter. They are all seated except 1st Twin, who enters last, clocks Angel, quickly writes out her sticker and then uncomfortably takes her seat. All are named. All are present.

Except Nanny, the matriarch, who is conjured up and impersonated by various family members when she speaks. The re-enactment of Nanny is always used as a tool to evoke reactions in each other.

Note: time is not linear but cyclical. This should be embraced with no attempt to literalise the setting. A scene may start in the present and shift into the past. The actors should embrace this, and not attempt to play young or old to justify it.

Angel locks the door.

The Brooks family are gathered to confront the truth and that is the end of it. Nobody can leave until the truth is attained.

Scenes should be played out within the circle, either sitting or standing, observed by the remaining members. The circle may or may not dismantle as the investigation goes on, but this should be entirely organic and in direct relation to what is happening between the Brooks. Rather, all choreography should be born out of psychological intention or story.

A slash / is a point of interruption. Dialogue in (*brackets*) is expressed non-vocally.

Characters

Angel
1st Twin
2nd Twin
Aunty L
Aunty J
Brotha
Couzin
Steve
Brian

Silence . . .

Angel *stands and addresses the family.*

Angel   It happened.
You don't want me to say it but it happened.
To me
OK fucking happened
To me
not them
that shit happened to me.
While you were all
playing
at being happy families
that shit was happening to me
so there it is –
believe it or not.
It's you that's gotta sleep at night
knowing what you know to be true –
it's you that's gotta
carry that truth around
in your heart
So . . .
Well? WELL? WELL?!

Beat.

1st Twin   Why do you persist on hurting on me?
I don't know what I have done to merit / this, why?

Angel   You all seeing this?

1st Twin   There are things, Angel,
things which we don't fully understand
at the time
when they're happening / to us.

Aunty L   An intellectual? Most people call me that / yeah.

2nd Twin   As if –

Angel   Fuck you fuck you / fuck you fuck –

Aunty L   Well, it's the truth.

1st Twin   If you behave like this you can go straight to your / room.

Aunty L   Your mother said that I could / have you.

Angel   My? Ha, that's funny – straight to my / listen.

1st Twin   We've come so far, daughter, from nothing to this!
He's done a lot
for us.

Aunty L   Ask her.

1st Twin   You too quick to forget what's been done for you
that's always been your problem.
Her perception
of things –

Brotha   It's like I've said –

Aunty L   Watch out for your brother / he's weak.

1st Twin   Has always been altered by her / up there Aunty
L –

Brotha   Come again?

2nd Twin   Nephew –

Aunty L   Do you know what subversion means?

Angel   Subtraction?

1st Twin   I mean look at the things
you've
we've
all of us got!

Brotha   (*Got*) work in the morning man!

Angel   You make me sick
you make me sick
you make me (*sick*).

1st Twin   Sweetheart please / stop.

Angel   You didn't have it in you to brandish on me
what you so freely and happily brandished on them
I'm that person – I see it now
I see that, Mummy,
but why me?
WHY ME AND NOT THEM?

Aunty J (*as Nanny*)   Forgive them, Father, for they know not
what they / do.

Aunty L   You always did her the best.

2nd Twin   Nanny.

––––––––––––––––––––––––

1st Twin *advances to* **Angel**.

1st Twin   Doing your hair
used to love doing your hair
in the bath
your beautiful hair.
Loose.
Loose long locks
falling down your back.

Angel   Yes?

1st Twin   Natural, *au naturel*,
everything about you was natural.

Angel   Natural?

1st Twin   Yes. Running a comb through your hair
was always a time of great tranquility for me
and you I hope?

Angel   You ran a comb through it?

Aunty L   She never ran a comb / trou it.

1st Twin   Yes! That shiny black, well-conditioned hair
of yours
Long thick and healthy.

Aunty L   Hmmm.

1st Twin   Not like mine.
Better than mine
Coolie
It was coolie
almost Indian in fact
which is strange
as I don't remember having any Indians

Beat.

In the family.
No, so I guess you're just unique
by default you're just unique
special!
Don't ever fool yourself into thinking that you aren't.
That in itself
Is an illusion
Princess /
a lie

Angel   Spare
me
the
bull
please

1st Twin   When you ran. Away that time, ran away.
And we were all worried
terribly worried
for you and your whereabouts
and safety.
Just that note, that little note you left, 'I'm going away',
like a call for help
a call for recognition
I understood we'd failed you when deciphering your note

in red crayon writing smudged
I remember thinking that I'd failed you.
And with the police cars out
the searchlights on and us all worried sick!
Your couzin welled up
and the silence, that eerie silence
while we waited –
when all the while – bless you – all the while
you were just around the corner at your 'mates'
who ratted you – out of friendship – ratted you
and well, I should of known back then
and maybe we wouldn't be here – where we are – now in
    all this (*trouble*)
Maybe this is one of those?

Couzin   One of those / what?

Brotha   Long time Emmanuel

1st Twin   Cries for help.

Angel *is stifled for a moment.*

Couzin   Time.

Brotha   What can I say man, it passes.

Couzin   It does at that.

Brotha   I never hear from you, I haven't heard from you
in a while?

Couzin   I'm here.

Brotha   Yeah, we all here

Couzin   Not all of us

Brotha   Nah?

Beat.

Couzin   That's why I'm here –

Brotha   Sit down man, shit, you just step trou the door
and not even / sit down yet!

Couzin   I'm wet.

Brotha   OK?

Couzin   From outside.

Brotha   Yeah well, look, what's new? You get big, ha?
You were never that big before!

Couzin   I eat 'nough.

Brotha   Good, that's good.

Couzin   Just blew up one day you know
blew
up.

Aunty L   Like his father.

2nd Twin   Oh what do you know?

Aunty L   Lots. Sis / lots.

Brotha   So what brings you round?

Couzin   Angel.

Brotha   Her.

Angel   (*What*) the fuck?

Couzin   Her yeah? That how you phrase it now?

Angel   It ain't no surprise!

Brotha   What is this?

Angel   Brotha.

Couzin   Her? The cat's mother and / all that?

Brotha   What you getting at, cozzy? I just sit down for
breakfast
What you eating? Let me get you suttin –
If you eating
If you always eating then you'll eat some more

Couzin   What's cooking?

Brotha   Pancakes.

Couzin   Oh go on then.

Brotha   That's more like it!

Couzin   Not too much sugar!

Brotha   It need sugar, cozzy,
you must know
and butter
and honey
and then a sprinkle a' flower.

Couzin   Why not . . .

Brotha   You see! You see? What I tell yer?

Couzin   She's asking after –

Brotha   See, it's like nothing changes.
My little cozzy drops by
And I have to educate him on the way of eating pancakes.

Couzin   I said she's asking after / Angel.
She's back for –

Angel   . . .

Brotha   Wait for the pan!
You have to wait for the pan to get hot
once it's hot then you crack the eggs
that's when you go in with the mix
but not until then.
So if you'd do me the kindness to wait until the pan's hot
'fore we start cracking eggs
It'd be much appreciated.
Couzin.

2nd Twin   My son.

1st Twin   You had a flair for fantasy Angel.
I always thought one of these days you'd make it to the stage –
they say some parts of the brain are more active than others –
you know like when they do studies . . . on sociopaths.

Angel   You calling me a sociopath?

1st Twin   No! No! God no! I'm saying you lack rationale,
and that could actually serve as a career
choice.

Couzin   Wow!

Angel   Lacking rationale?

1st Twin   Yes, rationale – but not empathy. We've both
retained that.

Beat.

Haven't we? . . . Haven't we?

Angel   You're the fuckin' sociopath.

Couzin   Shame!

2nd Twin   Emmanuel!

Couzin   What?

_____

Aunty J (*as Nanny*)   March Second. A Wednesday.
Weather overcast, but with talk of sunny spells later.
Favourite daughter
of the day

2nd Twin   Says who?

Aunty J   Wasn't it?

_____

Steve   I think we're having Chinese tonight!

Angel   Hmm.

Brotha   YES!

Steve   Chicken chow mein . . . special fried rice
chicken balls, in sweet and sour sauce.
Peking duck with steamed pancakes
spare ribs
hot pepper squid
lemon chicken with herb
chilli beef, treasure rice,
prawn crackers – and what else?

Beat.

Brotha   We getting all of that?

Steve   If you like?

Brotha   What kind of ribs?

Steve   Dry I think.

Brotha   Ha – why would you get dry ribs? Dry? / Nasty!

1st Twin   Go check on your sister –

Brotha   Why?

1st Twin   Would you just go and check on her please?

Beat.

Steve   I'll go –

1st Twin   He'll go like I've asked – won't you, son?

Brotha   Is she eating?

Beat.

Is she eating? Mum?

1st Twin   Yes.

Angel   Really?

1st Twin   No. Not with us, at the table.
So go take her up a menu and see what she wants –
You were fed –

Brotha   Man!

1st Twin   I beg your pardon?

Brotha   What?

1st Twin   (*What*) did you just say?

Brotha   I just said, that's pretty harsh.
See, sis.

Angel   See what?

Steve   1st Twin –

1st Twin   Well, do you want to join her? You can join her
if you want –
take up the menu and then join
her –

Brotha   No!

1st Twin   You mean you want to eat at the big table?

Brotha   . . . Yes . . .

1st Twin   Well, go and do as you're told.

Brotha   Yes, Mum.

Angel   HA!

1st Twin   Good boy.

Angel   Exactly!

Brotha   Whatever, man cha!

He gets up and pours himself some water having been found out.

Angel *persists.*

Angel   What was driving you?

1st Twin   You got through it, didn't you?

Aunty J (*as Nanny*)   *You'll dance just like the rest of 'em danced*
And you won't disappoint

Angel   What happened to you, back then? I mean really happened?

Aunty J (*as Nanny*)   When Nanny has friends round.

1st Twin   I've made choices that . . . I've had to make work.
It's as simple as that.
You'll learn –
that survival is all that matters and shame,
Is as good as (*death*).
You'll learn,
that how you are perceived when you walk into a room
is the highest currency you have.

Aunty J   Yes . . .

1st Twin   When you've –
Look, my scars may not be flesh apparent –

Angel   Are you for real?

1st Twin   Excuse me? I beg your / pardon?

Angel   You have it! Yes I see it now – you have violence!
You have your mother's violence!

Aunty J (*as Nanny*)   A sack a' shite the lot a' yah!

2nd Twin   I do 'er better than that.

Aunty L   She said that I could have you . . . back then . . .
She said that I could have you.

Angel   Really?

Aunty L   Your mother said I could have you. That's what
she said,

ask her yourself, she'll admit it
It was always on the cards, my having you.

Angel   Why would she say that?

1st Twin   I –

Aunty L   Until she felt better.

Steve   Why don't we all / just –

Aunty L   Quiet, Steve!

Angel   How would I or you of benefited from that?

1st Twin   We –

Aunty L   How?

Steve   There's no need to be aggressive /
L.

Aunty L   I SAID QUIET!

Aunty J   L!

Angel   Why would she think a transaction like that
woulda been approved / by me?

Aunty L   Calm yourself, Ange.

Angel   I'm calm, Aunty,

Aunty L   Listen

Angel   Don't tell me to listen, yeah? I'm hurting right now,
you know hurting.

Aunty L   I know –

Angel   What the fuck do you know, man, leave me alone.

Aunty L   Ange.

Angel   Alone –

Aunty L   Please.

Angel   Alone. Leave your niece alone.

She gets up frustrated.

Steve *attempts to comfort.*

Steve   We should talk
shouldn't we? It's been a while . . .
since we talked
and I always loved our conversations
they could go on for hours.
Couldn't they?
Couldn't they?

Aunty L   Ange.

Brotha   What, you never 'ear 'er
The first time? Leave 'er be.

Steve   What's up?
What's up?
Homie?
My home girl? Nah?
OK then, suit yourself.
If that's what you want?
If that's how you want it?
But that's the last time I run a comb through your hair –

1st Twin *coughs uncomfortably.*

Steve   That's the last time I undo any knots
like the ones you used to get in your stomach . . . remember?
Those wicked knots.
I'm telling you yeah friends!

Angel   You think . . .

Steve   Yes?

Angel   Incorrectly. But then you can always just / leave . . .
couldn't you?

Aunty L   Leave.

1st Twin   Steve's fine where he is.
Aren't you?

Steve   Am I?

Silence.

Brotha *attempts to change the mood drawing* **Couzin** *into flashback.*

Brotha   I swear, cozzy, we musta kill that boy twice –

Couzin   Oh no!

Couzin   My big foot –

Brotha   Your big foot –
As we saddled down the hill
Brixton Hill.

Couzin   On my Knight Rider bike –

Brotha   Which you left outside 1st Twin's house –

Couzin   I was shook, so scared to even bring it in
Dunbarton –

1st Twin   He could of brought it in /
Should of

Brotha   Innocence –

Angel   Where?

Couzin   There was a time –

1st Twin   You better leave that bike outside,
nephew –

Couzin   See!

1st Twin   Well . . .

Brotha   Wind in yer face, trees on either side,
them paths leading off in all directions –

Couzin   Tudor Close –

Brotha   Mmm – always wondered what that building was –

Couzin   Like suttin outta Stephen King –

Angel   I told you that!

Brotha   When?

Couzin   Then the prison –

Brotha   The prison!

Couzin   Used to walk past it on my way to school –

Angel   The two of us walked.

Couzin   No we didn't?

Brotha   Funny innit –

Couzin   Why?

Brotha   Funny 'cause –
all the while you were bopping to primary school,
Uncle P was barred up in a cell,
just over the wall.

Couzin   Was he?

Brotha   All the while, cozzy – all the while –

Couzin   Deep –

Brotha   Robbery –

Couzin   Just that?

Steve   Armed robbery –

Aunty J   Not exactly –

Couzin   Well, I've heard a' worse things –
you throw a stone out there it'd be hard to hit someone
with integrity –

Brotha   Out there?

Couzin   Or in here –

Brotha   Yeah?

Couzin   Juss kidding –

Angel   No he weren't were you?
Cozzy?

Beat. **Couzin** *is unable to fully endorse* **Angel***.*

Brotha   'S just a pile a' scheming suits, brov, trust!

Beat.

He weren't a bad person, in many ways I hear he was their
  saviour –

Couzin   Is it?

Brotha   Regular Robin Hood –

Aunty J   That's right / nephew.

Couzin   Shot himself on the foot –

Brotha   In –

Couzin   What?

Brotha   In the foot, cozzy, not on –

Couzin   Yeah . . .

Brotha   Looked after us though, when they had it –

Couzin   Put me through college, –

Brotha   Aunty J –

Couzin   And Uncle P –

Brotha   Nice of them . . . sorted me out / too –

Angel   I wasn't sorted –

Aunty J   You were definitely / sorted.

Steve   I sorted things / out.

Aunty L   It was me who / did the sorting out
after you took (*advantage*)

1st Twin   Mummy did the sorting / out

2nd Twin   The twins did the sorting!

Steve   What?

Angel   We'll get to that
We'll get to all of that!
Cozzy?

Couzin   One sec –

Brotha   Well –

Couzin   But he was always close to you.

Angel   Me?

Couzin   Him.

Brotha   Yeah. We should visit –

Aunty J   None a' you visited

Couzin   Break him out –

Aunty J   And after all a' that
what he gave

Angel   I visited

Aunty L   Yes darling
You visited lots

Angel   No I mean
I meant Uncle (*P*).

Angel *in her frustration repositions herself in the circle.*

Angel   Br-Brother . . . we need to –

2nd Twin *impersonates Nanny.*

2nd Twin (*as Nanny*)   June 6th. Sunny.

Brotha *ignores.*

2nd Twin (*as Nanny*)   Sunbaked concrete and Sunkiss orange drinks.
Favourite of the day . . . Jay –
I mean, sorry I meant L,
she's the favourite of the day, the rest a' yah can go to hell,
until the sun goes down, and resurfaces. Ask me / again then.

Aunty L   J does 'er better

Aunty J *and* **2nd Twin** *go over to the tea area outside the circle and make tea.*

Angel *initiates the flashback and then observes it forensically.*

Aunty J/Angel   Look at you –

2nd Twin   What?

Aunty J   You look well, sis.

2nd Twin   Thanks.

Aunty J   You really do.

2nd Twin   . . . You don't look bad yerself.

Aunty J   Face-lift –

2nd Twin   What?

Aunty J   Face-lift –

2nd Twin   Where?

Aunty J/Angel   On my face.

2nd Twin   Jay!

Aunty J   Fuckin painful . . . if you ever consider it?

2nd Twin   I'm fine, thanks –

Aunty J   Here –

2nd Twin   I can't!

Aunty J   Here – look, from here to here –

2nd Twin   For what? For why?

Aunty J   – had the money –

2nd Twin   Just that?

Aunty J   We can't all look eternally young –

2nd Twin   Ah – Oh God –

Aunty J   The fagz –

2nd Twin   Well?

Aunty J   The fagz are responsible for my demise.

2nd Twin   So stop! Simple as that, put down the Benson's and get on with your life.
For Christ's / sake.

Aunty J   'S not as easy as that / 's never been as easy as that for (*me*)

2nd Twin   Why? I don't see why (*not*), never been near a cigarette / in my life

Aunty J   Yer lucky. I have a different kind / of stress.

2nd Twin   – the smell / the stench –

Aunty J   A rare breed – a rare breed / a Brook –

2nd Twin   Or drink / never drunk much either.

Aunty J   A saint / I got a saint round for tea and biscuits / lucky me

2nd Twin   Don't be tetchy now – no need to be / tetchy

Aunty J   Not like your son –

2nd Twin   What about him?

Aunty J   He loves a puff.

2nd Twin   Does he?

Aunty J   Doesn't he?

Couzin *sparks up in the circle.* **2nd Twin** *clocks, then:*

2nd Twin   No. Not my son.
That must be someone else's son, you speaking of.

Aunty J   Sure, must be . . . someone else – I was thinking – of.

Beat.

So is he?

2nd Twin   What?

Aunty J   Is he?

2nd Twin   Yes?

Spit it out, Jay!

Aunty J   Settled?

2nd Twin   He's doing his thing.

Aunty J   But is he?
Settled yet?
Like we were all
by his age
settled?

2nd Twin   He's ambitious –

Aunty J   I know he is!

2nd Twin   Spends most of his time working.

Aunty J   In the closet?

2nd Twin   In the basement.

Aunty J   Oh?

2nd Twin   What the fuck is it you're tryina say?

Aunty J   A handsome young buck like that . . .

2nd Twin   Precisely.

Aunty J   Must be fighting them off!

2nd Twin   Non-stop!

Aunty J   From all sides?

2nd Twin   All quarters. Yes.

Beat.

Aunty J   L seems to think –

2nd Twin   Her?

Aunty J   Yes her – big sis –

2nd Twin   What?

Aunty J   Seems to think . . .

Angel *prompts* **Couzin** *to speak.*

Couzin   Clumsy?

Aunty L   My nephew.

Steve   Ange.

Angel   Move!

Aunty J   And with her extensive knowledge in these / things –

2nd Twin   I'm just as clever as her –

Aunty J   All things, she is wise in
she / felt –

2nd Twin   That's enough. I think. For one cup of tea.

Steve   Ange.

Aunty L   Ange.
Come sit 'ere
With / Aunty

Couzin   You get branded a thing.

Angel   I'm fine where / I am.
Branded?

Aunty L   Well.

2nd Twin   More then enough. Jay . . . anyways, how's
you and yours?

Aunty J   You mean? –

Couzin   And before you know it you become it.

2nd Twin   Is he out? Or still in the jail 'ouse?

Angel   Yes?

Aunty J   He's –

Couzin   Not 'cause you were that thing to begin with.

Angel   No . . .

Aunty J   I can't say

Couzin   Just that –

1st Twin   Ange.

Angel   What? / WHAT!

Aunty J   He'll be seeing / daylight soon.

Couzin   Erybody spectin suttin from you / and you don't
wanna disappoint.

Aunty J   Or ever again for / that matter . . .

Couzin   Suttin like / that.

2nd Twin   You'll go to waste.

Aunty J   I'll wait.

2nd Twin   You've always waited –

Aunty J   He's always looked after.

2nd Twin   No one's questioning your loyalties.

Aunty J   I can't tell him what to do?!

2nd Twin   Nobody's questioning that . . . as nobody's
questioning my / boy

Aunty L   What are you like?

Couzin   See?

2nd Twin   We all understand why you wait.
He did a lot for us back / then.

Aunty L   What?

Couzin   Like?

Aunty L   When you ain't pretending – that everything
is jiggy wid you – nephew?

Couzin   Ha?

Aunty L   You got your mother's airs. Her moist airs.
She mois' that woman believe.

2nd Twin   Hmm.

––––––––––––––––––––

Couzin   The doubts I have are ideas she's planted,
Aunty L –

Brotha   They've got in my head – they've got in your head –
that's what they do!

But anyway man – it all leads
back to her –

Couzin   Who?

Brotha   You know who I mean?

Couzin   Nanny.

2nd Twin   Mummy?

Brotha   She's the heart of all this confusion, 'trust' –

Couzin   On your head / be it –

Angel   First Saturday –

Brotha   Her manipulation runs deep –

Couzin   Exactly –

Brotha   Mmm . . . not in the men though / not the men.

Angel   What men?

Aunty L   Are you / for real?

Couzin   You think?

Brotha   Yeah . . . don't you?

Couzin   I asked you –

Brotha   Why?

Aunty L   Still / shook
As ever, Brotha

Brotha   Me?

Angel   Can I speak?

Couzin   You think you've come out of it unscathed?

Brotha   What?

Couzin   The family –

Brotha   Shut up man . . . how you mean?
Why you think I changed my name /
not all of us clinging this –

Aunty L   I was raised by intellectuals / But just me.

Angel   CAN I?

Brotha   Asked 'er who our / grandad was –

Aunty L   Hence my superiority –

2nd Twin   Complex.

Aunty L   What –

Couzin   – she say?

Brotha   Nuttin' much / just a passing fancy.

Angel   First –

Couzin   Fuckin deep –

Angel   I mean – / what I was meant to say was –

Brotha   Then all of this –

Couzin   Must stretch back further –

Brotha   Before Nanny.

Angel   Is –

Brotha   We'd be prime candidates for / Benetton.
Spring season.

Aunty J   Yours was darker / hence your darkness.

Aunty L   Mine?

Aunty J   Hers.

Brotha   I was gonna / write in.

Aunty L   Darkest

2nd Twin   I don't remember . . . freckles –

Aunty J   Mines was white / just a simple plain white.

Angel   Yours was?

2nd Twin   I never needed one –

Aunty J   Greek, he was Greek, but fair, hence / my features –

2nd Twin   A father? Never required it

Angel   A grandad / though?

Couzin   Exactly –

Aunty J   Coulda done / with one myself –

Brotha Don't watch that cozzy

2nd Twin For the aesthetic maybe / for the aesthetic.

Angel You listening!

Aunty J Just a mother –

Angel Aunty J?

2nd Twin We –

Angel 2nd Twin?

Aunty J A fully functioning mother would of been nice.

2nd Twin She –

Aunty J Let's not –

2nd Twin Had her moments –

Aunty J Ah?

2nd Twin Her rare moments of sober compassion.

Angel Nanny?

Aunty J Barely memorable, in amongst all the other shit She emptied on us –

2nd Twin Me –

Aunty J You?

Aunty L (*indicating* **Aunty J**) Her.

2nd Twin Me in particular, yes, and 1st Twin –

1st Twin Yes.

2nd Twin But most of all me –

Aunty J That's not how I? /
Since when were you the one of taken the brunt?!

2nd Twin You'd left, you'd gone!

Aunty J I'm the older – second eldest hence –

Angel   First (*sat*).

2nd Twin   Look, its not a competition /
I'm not tryina compete

Aunty J   Hence years a' shit
years a' brazen foul-mouthed shit /
years a' hurt
years a' heady humiliation
before you even touch dis planet
Sis –

2nd Twin   OK, yes, I get your point, I wasn't there
but she claims that
that was when she had her shit together
as it were.
In-tact.

So, in any case, your years before equal out mine spent –
    after you left

Aunty J   Escaped more like, ha . . .

2nd Twin   So when's he getting out?

Aunty J   I said? Didn't I say?

2nd Twin   You'll get cobwebs –

Aunty J   What?

2nd Twin   You know where –

Angel   FIRST SATURDAY OF THE MONTH!

Angel *regains the focus of the circle.*

Angel   Then every other Saturday –
then Saturdays –
then Fridays and Saturdays – you started leasing me out . . .
But always to Aunty L – always up to Wes' London –

1st Twin   You're spending the weekend with L – I'm
struggling –

Angel   First I was like cool! Aunty L's
the way kids do
when they get to be away from home
eat fast food and stay up late watching television
without getting told off –
but that was never how it went down – was it?
That was never the intention?

1st Twin   Like I said. It was a routine, we got into a rhythm.

Aunty L   Yes –

Angel   Some kinda offbeat fucking rhythm, coz as the
    regularity settled in
I realise I'm being groomed –
for someone else.
That these weekend trips to boarding school –
are so you can lay me
and my little brown skin off!
That L – and you –
were engaged in a sorta unspoken contract –
that benefited her and benefited you –

Aunty L   I was trying to / help!

Angel   Her cravings for a child and your burden!
Your wanting to start again
from scratch –
as you lowered to Steve and his manipulation

1st Twin   She's saying –

Steve   What? . . . What *is* she saying?

1st Twin   It's not good / Steve.

Angel   Out of sight – out of harm's way –
(*you*) couldn't bear the truth of it mother.
You couldn't bear the face that reflected your image, that's right!

First me – and then Brotha –
I see it now . . . it all so fuckin apparent . . .

Steve   What?

Angel   Let me tell you I ain't resting –
I ain't resting till I've burned down the walls of your flimsy
castle, I am on you – yah get me / on. You.

Steve   What? Hunny . . . what?

1st Twin   You didn't, did you?
Didn't . . .
I know you didn't.

Beat.

1st Twin   Did you?

Steve   . . . (*What?*)

1st Twin   'Cause that's not what 'we' do –
that's not what's done
in this family.
That kinda thing
That kinda warped fucked-up thing
will never be done
in ours – to ours.
Isn't it?

Beat.

Isn't it? . . .

Angel   Steve?

Steve   I don't know what you're getting at.

1st Twin   Good.

Steve   I don't know exactly . . . what it is . . . you're getting at?
1st Twin? . . . what is it you're getting at?

Beat.

1st Twin   She's got a vivid imagination, that girl.

Angel   Are you for real?

1st Twin   Always had a vivid –
heightened sense of reality.
Don't you think?

Brotha   Aha.

Steve   I have noticed that
on occasion
yes.

Aunty J   Me too.

Aunty L   J!

Aunty J   She has!

1st Twin   Part of her charm no doubt, yes,
But every now and then . . .

Steve   What, love?

1st Twin   Every now and then . . .
It spills.

Steve   Spills?

1st Twin   And here we are – you and me – all of us –
covered

Steve   What?

1st Twin   In all her –

Steve   Yes?

1st Twin   In all her . . . lies.

Angel   Tssss.

Aunty J   I never meant / lies.

Steve   Should I put the kettle on?

1st Twin   Yes. Yes. Did you?

Steve   What?

1st Twin   Fill it up?

Couzin *gets up in his frustration and exposes the circle.*

Couzin   TOO MANY SECRETS! A' too many secrets
in this family!

Brotha   Ma shalla –

Couzin   NOBODY WANTS TO SAY!

Nobody wants to say
how or who
or even if that 'ting' happened!

Brotha   What ting?

Couzin   All the things!

Brotha   Which. Thing. Exactly?

Angel   Say it . . .
Couzin / say it.

2nd Twin   Sit down, son.

Couzin   Sit?

Brotha   Which?

Aunty L   Nephew?

Brotha   Thing?

2nd Twin   Son!

Steve   Let him sit . . .

Aunty L   Oh you'd be happy for him to sit
this shit out!

Angel   Go on!

Brotha   What you saying, cozzy?

Couzin   What I gotta be first to actually say
It?

Angel   It?

Steve   Sit. Let the man
Sit.

Angel   SHUT UP, STEVE!

Steve   YOU WATCH YOUR TONE
YOUNG LADY!

Couzin *sits.*

Angel   Manuel . . . ?
M – (*Manuel*)?

Aunty J *stands and impersonates Nanny.*

Aunty J (*as Nanny*)   When I hand this over to you, it'll be up
to you to lead the family.
To take the reins.
To be an example.
You're the fairer one, you were always fairer then the others
you were always loved
I loved you the more.

Yeah, you'll be just fine,
It'll be left up to you to keep an eye on 1st Twin,
she needs you
They all need you
Just – pray to God, just
Almighty Father, after all I've seen and done,
Be watchful of the darker ones – be watchful of the darkers.

It's beside me
It's besides me
how dark they all came out when I'm so (*white*).

Protect them as I've protected you – I – I?
Where's L?

She always makes a fuss and then doesn't come to see me
Oh Lord it . . .
Tell 2nd Twin I love 'er
and I'm sorry but –
well, she never tidies up how she should when she comes.

I know I did wrong back then – was when I spilt
was when I spilt
hot burning fat all over my body
that was when I finally woke up!
When I was a bubby
you see when I was a bubba
they used to –
Lord Jesus they used to lock me in a draw about a foot by
    half a foot
It's no wonder I went off the rails.
But well, don't blame me don't blame me
at least I had yer
at least I birthed you out!
I can't say anyone else would.
There'd be no 'us' if it wasn't for me
and to top it all off
you'll never have to worry bout cancer
'cause we ain't got it in our veins.
So be grateful and go turn off the fridge . . .
That buzzing be giving me a headache

Aunty J   Yes, Mum. Of course, Mum. / Course.

Steve   When I knocked on your door that day.

1st Twin   Which day was (*that*)?

Steve   Dunbarton Road. Dunbarton.

1st Twin   Romantic.

Steve   I wouldn't call it romantic – I dunno if I'd call it /
romantic

1st Twin No?

Steve My coming to collect debts at your door.

1st Twin Endearing
to have the heart to
relinquish the debt
in favour of something far more valuable.

Steve Love. Is it 'cliché' to call it love?

1st Twin Call it what it is.
Was.

Steve Two minutes later we were having tea, two years later
    I proposed.

Beat.

1st Twin My children are (*black*).

Steve Gift. A gift from God.

1st Twin You didn't know, at the time, until later.

Steve A surprise no doubt – a surprise . . . but these
    things happen
life happens, and the baggage we have –

1st Twin Baggage?

Steve Well, you only wanted the one, right?
Unless I?

1st Twin Black ha . . .
My two brown children what a surprise!
Dunbarton grey –
Dunbarton damp . . . /
drab.

Angel *leaves the stage.*

Steve Protect. What needs protecting.
Wife.

1st Twin How do you? Oh Steve, she – (*Angel*) –
I don't know what I've done?!

Steve   Protect. I'll protect you – I'll protect her
from herself
from the things that harm her – and in turn . . .

Brotha   She really haft to bring 'im back?

1st Twin   Yes?

Steve   Keep everyone safe. Coz it's clear as crystal day,
the squalor you left and the burdens of
the past, will never return on my watch.

Ever.

1st Twin   Thank you. Thank you . . . thank you, Steve!

Steve   I'll have a / word.

Angel   It's two o'clock.

Brian   Yes?

Angel   In the afternoon.

Brian   And?

Angel   You already drinking.

Brian   Drinking yes – I'm drinking – so what's good?

Angel   What?

Brian   I'm askin' what's good innit – with you my daughter!
What's –

Angel   How many you had?

Brian   How –
What?
How many what?
Am I s'posed to have?
To of had
By now?
There's a riddle

If you can solve it – life!
You'd be better to –
you'd do well ta'
so well – hot today innit / hot

Angel   You're just!
Look at you!
Look!
IT'S NO WONDER!

Brian   What? Look at what?! What I'ma s'posed to be
    looking at?!
You want some money?
Is that it?
One second –

Angel   I'm in trouble.

Brian   Thought I had some, somewhere?
'Ad some –
In my –
Fuuuuck! Where my tings keep going?!

Angel   Trouble. There's trouble. I just thought I'd tell you
there's gonna be trouble.
So . . . well – It concerns you.
It's gonna concern you.
When it comes –

Brian   Trouble?! What's? What you done knaw?
What the bubble have you done knaw?!
School is it? School.
A school ting – with the teachers?

Angel   At home. With them. At home. With him. That /
    thing

Steve (*to* **Brotha**)   Trainers new.

Brian   What? What's going on? How's your mum?
She still asking after me? She still asking
after?

Steve   Anorak . . . new.

Angel   Steve –

Brian   Yeah – got what she wants now / a whitey – a tick-all-the-boxes whitey

Angel   Dad!

Steve   Levis new – brand new.

Brian   Wait a minute – you tryina tell me –

Angel   If you'd let me!

Steve   The brand new you.

Brian   Your brotha?

Steve   Son.

Aunty L   Step (*son*).

Brian   Is this to do with him?
The like what never visits!

Angel   Bro (*ther*) what the fuck's this got to do with him?
Why has this always gotta come back to
him?! Why –
why are we back here talking 'bout . . . man forget it.
Forget you – just – aaahhhh!

Brian   Swearing? Swearing is it now? I'm just saying –
is it about him – coz it normally is, isn't it?

Steve *is uncomfortable as* **Angel** *has the circle fully engaged.*

Angel   Sit down

Brian   Ah?

Angel   Sit.

Brian   OK?

Angel   Listen.

She cracks open a drink and hands it to him.

Angel　When I'm in the / (*bath*)

Steve　OK – OK, SO THIS IS HOW THE GAME WORKS!

Aunty L　Sing it, Steve –

Steve　'Scuse me?

Aunty L　You know, sing it! Tell it!

Steve　I will, if you'd let me –

Aunty L　Maybe I've got a better one? Ange?

Angel　Aunty's games are the best –

Aunty L　Exactly –

1st Twin　But Steve has a game . . . let Steve do his game, then we can pitch in after – Steve –

Aunty L　Well, it's your house –

Aunty J　Is it?

1st Twin　What do you mean, is it?

Aunty J　I'm just saying did you look into what I said? about buying it –

1st Twin　Steve's / looking (into it)

Steve　RIGHT! Here's how the game goes,
we spilt into pairs
and in our pairs
we have to decide on what kind of animal we are,
say a penguin or a gorilla or –

Couzin　Shark?

Brotha　Iss not an animal, cozzy, it's a fish –

Steve　Quite right, fowl or mammal preferably,
you're gonna need something which makes sound –

Aunty L   Cluck cluck cluck! Like a chicken, Steve? Chicken?
Cluck cluck!

Steve   Exactly, so we make up a version of that sound,
me and my partner, then one of us leaves
the room, blindfolded whilst the other stays –

Aunty L   Blindfolded as well –

Steve   No . . . that's not what I said –

Aunty L   Well, hurry up then, Steve –

Couzin   Sounds complicated?

1st Twin   Ssshhhhh!

2nd Twin   Don't tell my boy to sshhh!

1st Twin   Well –

Steve   So what happens next is, the blindfolded partner
    has to come back in,
and find their original partner,
by using the sound they made up together –
but the obstacle is – everybody
else in the room has to imitate that sound –
meaning you'll have to listen very carefully –
meaning you'll really have to tune into your partner's sound,
to be able to find them.

Brian   A wha' de rass?

1st Twin   I'm game!

Steve   Great! Find partners –

1st Twin   2nd Twin I'll go with you –

2nd Twin   I'm going with Jay –

Aunty L   I'll go with Ange –

Angel   I'm going with Mum –

1st Twin   I'm going with Steve –

Steve   I'm going with Brotha –

Aunty L   I'll go with Couzin –

Couzin   OK, Aunty L –

Steve   That leaves –

Angel   Me and Mum.

1st Twin   Me and Angel?

Steve   That's right, let's start!

Angel   What do you want to be, Mum?

1st Twin   You choose –

Angel   What about . . . ?

1st Twin   Seen as you cornered me into it –

Angel   Cornered?

1st Twin   Yes, cornered. Like you normally do.

Angel   OK?

Beat.

What about penguins?

1st Twin   Vultures it is then.

Angel   Vultures?

1st Twin   Scavengers, yes.

Beat.

1st Twin   . . . So let's make up the sound.

_____

Angel   You made me the butt of all your jokes. We'd never talk.
There were no words shared
between mother and daughter?

1st Twin   Mother?

Aunty L *as Nanny. Summoned by* **Angel**.

Aunty L (*as Nanny*)   Yes?

Angel   And daughter.

1st Twin   Share . . .

Aunty L (*as Nanny*)   Steve . . .

1st Twin   What?

Angel   I am also a mother now.

Aunty L (*as Nanny*)   Steve . . .

Angel   That makes you grandmother, Mum,
A grand(*mother*)

Coz you were ill weren't you
Ill
When you had me.

Aunty L (*as Nanny*)   You do what you can to keep hold of (*him*)
You do what you can
this time.

Angel   And so Bri ran out

Brian   I never ran.

Aunty J (*as Nanny*)   To keep hold
of someone good
of something solid.

Angel   Tried but couldn't hack your
Post-(*natal*)

Brian   Your mudda just –

Aunty J (*as Nanny*)   Steve
Let him stretch his legs a little
If he needs to . . .
but keep hold
he has my blessing.

1st Twin   Yes . . .

Aunty J (*as Nanny*)   Steve has my blessings.

Nanny's endorsement of **Steve** *hangs heavy on the Brooks for a beat.*

Couzin *stands, raises his hand and makes a statement.*

Couzin   You know, everybody has this impression of me –
I'm the favourite,
I'm the shining beacon,
But my gift
Brotha
Is that my
capacity to hide is much stronger then yours.
I admire your recklessness
your rage always wore the seat-belt of integrity.

Me? On the other hand, the rage I feel in my heart is polluted.

Brotha   How yah mean?

Couzin   Skewered . . .

2nd Twin   Son?

Couzin   As a boy I remember – we had this Siamese cat
called Blue – because its eyes were electric –
blue. Anyway, when everyone was out I'd terrorise that cat,
I'd chase it with a broom – I'd
torment it . . . and then afterwards, I'd caress it, I'd hold it
    dear to my chest.

I'd feel a great sense of shame and guilt as I would hold it . . .
I look back at that routine, and
I honestly wonder if it was learned behaviour?

Brotha   . . . Kids do that kinda / stuff –

Couzin   I have sociopathic tendencies.
Periods where I feel zero empathy.
I find / it deeply worrying
When it happens.

Aunty L   It's OK for you to be whatever / you want to be.

Couzin   I realise that my own mother
robbed my of my right to emote . . .
I see now that her volatile fits took precedence
over my journey into manhood.

Aunty L   People say that you should hold back . . .
what you truly are – nephew / but it's OK –
to be seen.

Couzin   I reserve a small grain of hatred for my (*mother*) –
just a small one . . .
Do you have any / theories
on that?

Aunty L   There's no shame in being seen,
if you know what I mean?

Couzin   Do you know what it's like
to crush your father's wedding ring
in a nut cracker?

Brotha   No?

Couzin   It's exhilarating.

Aunty L   If we can't be seen
in this life, then 'when' and 'where' can we ever be seen?

Couzin   I idolised your eyes.

Brotha   Shut up, man –

Couzin   Them hazel eyes –

Brotha   'S just eyes innit –

Couzin   No, people wanted answers for my blackness –
answers I never had to hand.

Brotha   Bun them / bun them to ashes –

Couzin   How was it you got to get their eyes?

Brotha   Nature – like you said –

Couzin　You resented your own beauty made yourself
coarse –
like the concrete / like the road

Brotha　What? / Now you talking all kinds a fluff man –

Couzin　Everything narrower – stream-lined –
a stream-lined version of / me

Brotha　You got looks man shit!

Couzin　It's not about looks – it's –
I look like him what I've never met –
my / father –

Brotha　We look like brothers – every one used to say
We / looked like brothers –

Couzin　But you wasted it Brotha – you fuckin wasted
　　your beauty –
your beauty would of been
better served in my eager hands –

Brotha　You want this face?

Couzin　Not now.
It doesn't hold the same weight / now.

Brotha　You saying I no longer got it? /
Da fuck you getting' at?

Couzin　I'm saying there comes a point when a man has to
display his worth –

Brotha　I'm a father –

Couzin　OK –

Brotha　I brandish love on my children!
Each one of mine knows what they came from!
Who – they came from!

Couzin　No one's questioning / that.

Brotha   Yeah? So what the fuck is you want Couzin?
If I was hard on you –
it was to make you
strong / like you are.

Couzin   Angel.

Brotha   Like you've become /
like I see you –
stood there in front of me –
rooted to the ground.

Couzin   Angel. Angel. Ange –

Brotha   YES! ANGEL! FUCKING ANGEL! . . .
Where did we leave that?

Steve   Why would I wanna leave?

Couzin   We stood and watched / it happen.

Steve   I've got the run of the place . . .

Brotha   We had no clue / as to what was going on!
WE WERE YOUNG!

Steve   Your mum's over the moon.
I've laid foundations / here.

Brotha   I WAS YOUNG!

Steve   Have you seen the decor of the new house?
'Nouveau riche'. Its much bigger than Dunbarton, isn't it?

Angel   I don't care.

Couzin   She was our duty / is 'still' our duty –

Steve   We're what you call 'civilised'.
I've taken your mum to higher levels /
she exudes – authority
and class.

Brotha   Listen, Couzin, yeah, whatever's propelled you
to your 'Christian crusade' –

Steve   She has a 'new' hop in her step.

Brotha   Whatever /
sudden waking guilt –

Steve   It's undeniable / have you seen it?

Brotha   Whatever insomnia / leave that at the fuckin door –

Steve   A woman
walking the steady track
where the pavements are paved with gold.
There's something happening here. A renaissance –
you know what that means? A rebirth.
But you and your brother –

Angel   What about us?

Steve   I'd just hate for you to get left behind, swept aside,
   in the new currents.

Beat.

So fall in line . . . fall in line, Angel, and go run me a bath . . .

Angel   Why?

Steve   Well, why do people take baths? To clean off
   for fuck sake –
what is up with you?
I'll run it then.

Beat.

I'll run it.

———————————————

Brotha   We gonna draw blows? Let's start from scratch.

Couzin   Sure.

Brotha   Are you gay?

Couzin   What?

Brotha   You heard.

Couzin   That's ridiculous –

Brotha   Well?

Couzin   No.

Brotha   Not even a little bit?

Couzin   Absolutely not.

Brotha   We've established that.

Couzin   Established.

Brotha   Good. Not that I ever thought it / I mean –

Couzin   'Cause I'm trendy?

Brotha   What?

Couzin   But basically 'cause I'm trendy?

Brotha   Are you for real?

Couzin   Risqué when I dress –

Brotha   Not really –

Couzin   Come on, cozzy, I see yer eyes glance –

Brotha   Well . . .

Couzin   I like fashion, what can I say?

Brotha   You got style –

Couzin   Ain't my fault –

Brotha   Aha.

Couzin   And I'm creative –

Brotha   We both are –

Couzin   Live a life of a creative.

Brotha   . . .

Couzin   And I'm open. To things . . . not to them exactly – but

Brotha   Rah?!

Couzin   You would accept it, though . . . me?

Brotha   Come again?

Couzin   If I was?

Brotha   You saying you are?

Couzin   I'm saying . . . theoretically speaking

Brotha   You know how I feel about them tingz there, cozzy –

Couzin   There we are then.

Brotha   Cool.

Couzin   Nothing to worry about.

Brotha   Absolutely nothing.

Couzin   So?

Beat.

Where you going with the gay thing? Seems a bit flimsy.
Last-ditch attempt / at something.

Brotha   L.

Couzin   Oh, OK . . .

Brotha   Aunty L.

Couzin   What of 'er?

Brotha   Wicked witch in a de wess London –

Couzin   You could say –

Brotha   What?

Couzin   The woman has issues.

Aunty L   There are places you can go, to safely encounter
the unknown –

Brotha   Right, let's do the math.
When we used to go around there
and she'd show us them subversive movies – what was
'actually' going on?

Couzin   What movies?

Brotha   *Rocky Horror Show*, man, and fuckin Prince, 'Purple
Rain'!

What was actually going on?

Couzin   Recrea / tion.

Brotha   Recruitment!
Brain-wash tings – she was on a brain-wash ting –
tryina normalise that kinda cross-gender perversion –

Aunty L   Dive in –

Couzin   Look –

Aunty L   An artist has to be / free!

Brotha   So now you see?

Aunty L   With creativity comes / openness.

Couzin   You blaming *Rocky Horror Show* for the failings of
your sister?

Brotha   No! No! That's not / what I'm saying!

Aunty L   His fear can't / become yours.

Brotha   See, this is what they do, cozzy –
the women in this family!

Aunty L   You have to tread your path / the one that's been
laid out in front of you

Brotha   But OK, let me finish the equation.
You went into the arts. You're what they call a video artist.

Your work is . . .
Well I wouldn't
say I know what it means –
I think you use way too many urinals –
but that's beside the point, you made it!
You made it out there and I respect that –
with that come respec' . . .
but behind
your back, while you signing your press release forms
and clinking wine with the intelligentsia –
who's creating falsities?
Who's putting greys on your bolded black?

Aunty L   You'll struggle without my / backing.

Brotha   On cozzy's 'sexuality'
who's fabricating spots
from their own image . . .
who's planting the
malignant seed of doubt?
Within this family?
Who?

Couzin   L.

Brotha   Say what?

Couzin   Aunty L.

Brotha   OK . . . OK, here we go . . . who had to draw it
    outta Angel?
Who / had to draw the accusation out?

Aunty L   What's happening, Angel? At home?

Brotha   From Ange? Who took 'er on long canal walks,
where they'd feed the pigeons / and when
they'd done feeding the pigeons –

Aunty L   Home, Angel, what's happening at home?
With them?

Angel   How do you mean?

Brotha   Start to feed her mind
like she does, wi' her shit
And discuss new living / arrangements?

Aunty L   Are things happening?

Brotha   So if we align the / accusations –

Aunty L   Because Shamika'
My frien'

Brotha   About what you get up to 'after hours' –
If we are to take / that

Aunty L   Yer Aunty's friens
just run in all flustered

Brotha   And align it with the other accusations – /
   made about Steve –
where do we end up?

Aunty L   And she's saying – that

Brotha   What
number do we end up with?

Aunty L   Things are happening . . .

Brotha   Can we have one truth / without the other?

Aunty L   But I can't / say it for you . . .

Brotha   Coz, for me . . .

Aunty L   All I can say is . . . some people aren't well.

Brotha   All I see is the same 'one' person,
behind the 'both' / lies.

Aunty L   And they can do things – you know / things . . .

Brotha   That's the sum of my calculations . . . unless / you
coming up with suttin else?

Aunty L   So what I'm saying is . . . are there 'things'
happening?

Angel   Yes.

Aunty L   There are things happening.
Things are happening, aren't they?
With Steve?
Happening, yes?
Happening.
He's inappropriate. Isn't he?
With you?

Angel   He's –

Aunty L   Yes?

Angel   He's . . . he says he's one of my closest friends.

Aunty L   Yes. Yes! But look – you need to say it . . .
I can't say it for you.
That ain't gonna stand up, is it?
And if you 'don't' say it . . . he may well do it again.
    To others . . . so say it.

Brotha   Cozzy?

Aunty L   Say it, Angel.
Say it. Like you said it to Shamika – no one's gonna be angry
with you . . .
Only if you 'don't' say it.

_____

The claustrophobia is at an all high. **1st** *and* **2nd Twin** *and* **Steve**
head over to the tea area.

Angel   . . . Steve's –

_____

1st Twin   Chrome –

2nd Twin   Lovely.

1st Twin   Embossed.

2nd Twin I love the depth –

1st Twin All along the skirting boards.

2nd Twin Both floors?

1st Twin Just the top floor to begin with.

2nd Twin Oh sis!

1st Twin Flesh orange –

2nd Twin For the bathroom?

Steve We were thinking for the bedroom.

1st Twin Were we?

Steve Weren't we?

2nd Twin In any case, oh sis!

Steve Floorboards –

1st Twin Varnished –

Steve On the bottom floor.

2nd Twin Day room –

Steve Day room? How'd you mean?

2nd Twin Day room . . . day room, Steve.

Steve Dining room, you mean?

2nd Twin A room, specialising in daylight!

Steve Oh . . . I see, a sort of made-up term?

2nd Twin If you like, Steve. If you like.

Beat.

2nd Twin Banisters.

1st Twin Oak?

2nd Twin Is this? Oh sis, I love the tones, look at the tones!

Steve   Chinkapin oak.

1st Twin   A rare oak.

2nd Twin   You mean?

1st Twin   Of the rarest kind.

Steve   It grows in shallow soils –

1st Twin   Tea?

2nd Twin   Tea! Yes teas all round, I think – or even
Chardonnay?

Steve   It's early –

2nd Twin   To toast your house, Steve.

1st Twin   Watch the walls.

Steve   Sorry?

1st Twin   The walls, Steve!
The walls!
With your hands . . .
You'll soil it
With your . . . (*hands*).

Steve   Well look . . . I'ma just leave yous two to it.

2nd Twin   Righto! Righto, Steve.

Steve *leaves.*

Angel   Please . . .

2nd Twin   Where is she?

_____

Angel   Listen

1st Twin   L's. She's at L's
Lord give me / peace.

Aunty J   You carry our hopes.

Couzin   What?

Aunty J   In your / heart –

Angel   I need you to / listen
To me.

Aunty L (*to* **Couzin**)   It was a pleasure having you /
whenever I had you.

Angel   For a change
For one / second –

Couzin   That's a bit extreme –

Aunty L   You were funny / always getting into accidents.

Aunty J   You carry the hopes of this family in your heart –

Angel   Insteada humming to your natural / rhythm.

Aunty L   Although you have your / mother's guile.

Angel   Steada taking on board what every one else is /
saying.

Couzin   What dyou mean?

Angel   Feeling / feigning.

Aunty L   Her acute ability to evade the question.

Aunty J   You'll put it on the map –

Couzin   Our name?

Aunty J   Exactly

Couzin   That bastardised name
Wi' all of its delusion /
Inherited from a stranger

1st Twin (*to* **Brotha**)   Do you like it?
The idea behind is that /
well, I shouldn't be encouraging this.

Aunty J   Embrace it. It's unique / it makes you unique.

Aunty L   She love you, I'll give 'er that
that I will give 'er.

Aunty L   Don't expect me to forget all the other shit
that's been
stapled to you
unawares.

Couzin   Like?

Aunty L   Rest your head, nephew . . . we'll get to that later.
Have you spoken to Angel recently? / She
needs you, now more then ever, you do realise that don't you?

1st Twin   But the idea is, you get together
You and the / others
And re-create famous wars

Angel (*to* **Brotha**)   Insteada conveniently staying neutral
Insteada turning your back on what concerns you most /
You, yes you, bro!
Insteada doing all that, I need you to listen –

1st Twin   You use your miniature tanks, planes,
    helicopters, battleships
to re-create famous wars in history.
They're / quite the rage – they really are
and you always loved your Scalextric.

Angel   – to 'me'
I need you take on board what 'I'm' saying
what I've sat you down to / hear
what's about to pierce – as it's steadily been piercing me –
trou the fucking heart

1st Twin   I'm worried about your sister
Son

Brotha   Why?

Angel   While you playing happy families – me
Me! I'ma need you to listen!
To me!

Brotha   OK sis / wa gwarn?

1st Twin   Your sister – I'm worried about your sister
Son –

Brotha   What – why?

1st Twin   I'm not asking you to take sides –

Angel   You listening?

1st Twin   But you will always stand by your mother.

Brotha   I'm – / I'm listening, yes!

1st Twin   Won't you?
Won't you?

Brotha   What she done now?

Angel   Good.

1st Twin   Promise / me!

Angel   Him.

Brotha   What?! OK – yeah, what's wrong, man?!

Angel   Steve.

1st Twin   She's sick and needs our help.

Aunty L (*to* **Angel**)   Come over
you should come over to mine
come over
I think it's time, don't you?
You came over?
Yes?

Weren't you meant to be coming up?
Last weekend – from last weekend I was sat here
we were sat here waiting for (*you*).

Angel   I drew you a picture.

Aunty L   A picture? For me? You hear that. Jay, she drew
    she drew me a picture!
Me.

Aunty J   What?

Aunty L   There's – we've got things for you,
there are things up here – waiting for you – presents
just for you and no one else
for you to open.
My sweetheart niece
daughter.

1st Twin   Angel!

Angel   Mum?!

Aunty L   Yes? I'm / here

1st Twin   Come off the phone
now
And stop rinsing up the bill!

Aunty L   Angel?

Beat.

Can I have her?
I'll have her
If you want
It'd be really nice
If I could have her
It would mean a great deal to me, sis,
If I could have her

Silence.

1st Twin   'Av er –

Aunty L   What?

1st Twin   Have. Her.

Aunty L   Your mother said that I could have you?

Angel   . . .

Aunty J *as Nanny.*

Aunty J (*as Nanny*)   Our Father –

Couzin   She swap alcoholism for Catholicism and all what's been done forgotten?
Everything suddenly jiggy?

Aunty J (*as Nanny*)   Hmmm.

Angel *observes the re-enactment intensely.*

1st Twin   There's nothing left to do with that girl.

Beat.

1st Twin   It makes no sense to me –

2nd Twin   Evil –

1st Twin   You think?

2nd Twin   Evil.

1st Twin   Who evil? What?

2nd Twin   Story in the paper – beheading thingy –

1st Twin   Are you listening? Are you listening to me? 2nd Twin?!

2nd Twin   Yes!

1st Twin   Why do you think Angel's so set?!

2nd Twin   Sis – please – don't worry yer head with that
now!

1st Twin   I can see it, I've always seen it in her eye /
vengeance –

2nd Twin   She's just a girl – she's your girl – I mean –
what do you want me to do about it?

1st Twin   I'm not asking for / you too –

2nd Twin   They look at me – they look at me and see you.
They associate everything they've had
with you – with me / on me!

1st Twin   You're my twin!

2nd Twin   I know, but that's not the point!

1st Twin   I've always been there for yours,
we've always / made Couzin a part of what was happening
    in our house!

2nd Twin   I'm not questioning that!

1st Twin   You forget, 2nd Twin, when the fridge was
    empty,
when times were hard – when you were
scraping through – who knocked on the door?
Who came over with the food?
Who mopped up the mess? After you decided to / (*top*)
I mean what would of happened, 2nd Twin?
If you actually succeeded in your plan?

2nd Twin   This isn't about that?! Hold on!
HOW DARE YOU!
This has nothing to do with that! /
How did we get from this to that?!

1st Twin   Me.
He would of fell to me.
Yours would of fell to me!
And I would of looked after, groomed – nurtured and fed!

That! Which selfishly you left behind!
The whole thing's connected!
I'm not tryina – throw – it – that – back in your face,
but you have to understand that Steve
would of been the one to steady the ship
to hold it all together
like he has – does, and hopefully always will!

But this thing which she's saying is true!
I can't buy!

Beat.

1st Twin   What's that look?

2nd Twin   I don't need to tell you what you already know.

1st Twin   You think he – ?

2nd Twin   I don't think nuttin, sis. It's not for me
    to have an opinion on.
But if you want me – need to me to have her.
Then I will.
But deal swiftly and safely, sis . . . coz this situation you're in –
    we're in –
Well, you know what I'm saying.
Be solid certain, 'fore you act on any impending impulse.
1st Twin.
You know in your heart what's true . . . and why and how
    and where.
It's in your hands, sis. She's in your hands.
But whatever decision you make.

Brotha   Boy . . .

2nd Twin   I'll back you.

Angel   Shit.

Brotha   I don't really know what to say to that, sis
I don't really know what to say, you know, sis

I don't really know what to say you know, sis
I don't really know what to say you know, sis
to that
What you just tol' me
I don't really know what to say?

Angel   I'm not interested in words.
Words don't got no hold here
DO
Its what you are going to do about it
DO!

Steve   Go upstairs.

Angel   Ha?

Steve   You didn't hear me?

Angel   Why?

Steve   Brush your teeth it's time for beddy-byes.

Angel   Ha?

Steve   You heard me.

Angel   You've gotten fat.

Steve   What?

Angel   And bald.

Steve   Where?

Angel   What do you mean, where? There and there. Derr –

Steve   Carry on –

Angel   Just an observation.

Steve   Carry on and see what you get –

Angel   What's that then?

Steve   When you push your (*luck*). Look, can you just go upstairs.

Angel   Sweat.

Steve   Ah?

Angel   All over your body . . . like a soggy white mass of −

Steve   That's it!

He chases her round the circle.

Angel   No please!

Steve   Too far − too too far − girls gettin' gobbled!

Angel   AAHHHHHH!

She bites his finger hard. It draws blood.

Steve   Fuck! Fuck, you drew blood.

Angel   Don't ever put your hands on me again, without permission.

Beat.

Angel   Now I'm ready to brush my teeth.
Now I'm ready.

———————————————

Brian *intervenes from outside the circle.*

Brotha   What's the rush?

Angel   Ready . . .

Brian   Sit down, son . . . take a pew . . .

Beat.

Brotha   Yeah?

Brian   Now your sister's saying some things . . .
She came round and said some things . . . and the
implications of these things son, are serious . . . they're
    very serious −
She came around here distraught, flying off the handle as
    she does,
but the truth of the matter is −

she came around making accusations of the kind which –
    if they are true –
put us all in a complex position –

He takes a sip from his drink.

The things she said, were so harrowing and bizarre

He takes another sip.

That I had to get her to say them twice over –
after which to be honest, I felt riddled son.
I felt sick –

Brotha   What she saying? Things about me?

Brian   She's saying that there's things going on in the house
32 Kato Road – things going on, son
what d'you make of that?

Brotha   I can't say I seen much going on, other than
    the usual –

Brian   What's that then?

Brotha   Creating a stir, to get everyone's attention.

Brian   A stir . . . she still causing stirs?

Brotha   All day every day.

Brian   Now what makes this grey is that we all know your
sister –
has a thing against your mum –
I'm not gonna beat around the bush – she's told lies in the
    past –

Brotha   That she has, Dad –

Brian   But then again so have you –

Brotha   When?

Brian   Well, like now?

Brotha   You think I'm telling porkies?

Brian   Well, are you?

Brotha   I just said – I ain't seen much innit –

Brian   But do you look –

Brotha   When?

Brian   Have you been looking! Have you been looking out! For her, like you should?

Brotha   She's my sister innit.

Beat.

Brian   There's some Yardies I know, son, I know them
    from Yard –
Kingston, Jamaica, and there's a version of this story
where 'he'
let's just say 'he' for now,
steps out of his moneylending castle and gets shot up
till 'im blud clart good and buried in the ground . . .

He takes another gulp.

That's one version and when we talking what we talking now –
that's something we have to consider –
them whiteys, when they get their mitts on our kind,
they like to meddle – I'm talking about the men . . .
Look at the news, you been watching it – look at all the butter-
    wouldn't-melt celebrities – getting named and shamed –
Look at even the politicians, son –
you have to look at these things . . .
and they all have the same unassuming vibe,
them all have the same – legitimacy.
As Steve.

He takes another sip.

. . . So what I'm saying is . . . what I'm saying to you, son,
quite simply is, are there things
happening, we need to be concerned about?

Brotha   Ask Mum innit . . . if you want the truth ask Mum –
coz I ain't saying nuttin. Not for me to
say.

What? You never bring any gifts this time? You normally
bring suttin.

Brian   And to think I call you son.

Brotha   Call me Bro.

The Brooks family are standing around the room. **Angel** *is escorted in
by* **Steve**, *blindfolded. He takes her to the middle of the room and spins
her round three times. Everybody including* **1st Twin** *changes positions
in the room.* **Angel** *then begins to make her distinct vulture sound.
Everybody imitates the sound.* **Angel** *sifts through people trying to
distinguish her mother's vulture sound. They are overpowered by the
communal vulture sound.* **Angel** *is drawn by a certain quality of sound.
She makes her way over to the sound, sure that this is the sound she
conceived with her mother.*

Angel   Found you!

But the person she has found is **Aunty L. Angel** *removes her blindfold.*

Angel   Oh . . . I thought you were my mother.

Aunty L   Did you, darling?

Aunty J   I'm buying all the nieces and nephews cars.

2nd Twin   OK?

Aunty J   I thought it would be nice for them to have a set
of wheels.

2nd Twin   I'm not sure Couzin's passed his test yet.

Aunty J   Well, when he does, you tell him to come to me . . .
and Uncle P

and we'll buy him his first car –
cash – no higher finance – none of that shit –

2nd Twin   Great –

Aunty J   Something he can call his own.

2nd Twin   He has an abundance he can call his own –

Aunty J   Be that as it may . . . he's important –

2nd Twin   You don't have to remind me of my son's
importance –

Aunty J   He's important to the family.

2nd Twin   Get to the point –

Aunty J   I am, that's what I'm saying . . . he's got talent.
I've identified it
and he needs backing, there's
no point backing those who don't have talent –

2nd Twin   What about Brotha?

Aunty J   He has talent, yes . . . and an affiliation with
destruction –

2nd Twin   Affiliation?

Aunty J   Or should I say penchant –

Beat.

I've been taking elocutions lessons . . . can you tell?

2nd Twin   . . . Erm yeah . . .

Beat.

Aunty J   And there's the TV, if you need it.

2nd Twin   We have a TV –

Aunty J   A bigger one – plasma – 55 inches –

2nd Twin   – Drop it round then –

Aunty J   We're up grading to 75 –

2nd Twin   Good for you, sis . . . good for you . . .

Beat.

Aunty J   It's important, 2nd Twin, to give him the chances
we never had.

2nd Twin   I know.

Aunty J   To be excessive . . . when you look out there at
the people
who succeed – they have backing.
So I'm just saying – OK, you've done well, you're doing
a great job,
but he can't always come to you . . .
There'll be things he can come to me for –

2nd Twin   We appreciate your help –

Aunty J   But the boy's too curious –

2nd Twin   How?

Aunty J   He's just too idealistic – at least he thinks he is –

2nd Twin   He has goodness.

Aunty J   He has goodness, but he also has rage. The kind
that goes inwards,
so just keep an eye.
We wouldn't want our prize asset getting mixed up
in the wrong kind of thing.
If we land at least one child on the moon – it'll be enough –
to secure our name . . .
it'll be worth it – it will shed light . . . you know – we can
say for all our . . . (*pain*)
that at least one succeeded . . . at least one – landed . . .
If he succeeds . . . we all succeed.
So just sway him . . . from meddling in stuff
what don't concern him and his livelihood –

You can't save everyone can you?

2nd Twin   No.

2nd Twin   The truth is overrated.

Couzin   How can you say that?!

2nd Twin   People put too much weight on truth –

Couzin   I need to know, there are things I need to know –
About me about Ange
things which will give me an identity / a
center

2nd Twin   You have an identity without those things, son,
that's how I raised you –

Couzin   Why did you tear up his letters . . . he sent letters –

2nd Twin   Yes, he (*your dad*) sent letters – yes – I tore them
up –
those letters weren't for you, son – that –

Couzin   And wait, so how did you come to that conclusion –
they were addressed to me –
meant for
me –

2nd Twin   You're a Brook – and that's the end of it –

Angel   There's never been an end to it –

1st Twin   She's not herself –

Angel   So that's why I'm here –

2nd Twin   I've protected you before – like I'm protecting
you now –
So please, son . . . stop this search,
It's doing nobody – especially yourself – any good –

Couzin   It's not as simple as that.

2nd Twin   What you don't know doesn't harm you –

Couzin   Flimsy fucking idealistic babble –

2nd Twin   What has he provided? Apart from the
  equipment, dare I say it?
You are my son! The man's
a diabetic! Is there any of that mark on you?
Is there any of that – decay on you?

Couzin   No –

2nd Twin   Exactly no – 'cause it's my blood –
my genetics – my nurturing that has
given you your breeding – not him . . . not (*Darren*).

1st Twin   She's not been herself for / a while –

Angel   Do you see?

1st Twin   I can't say she's ever been herself /
my daughter, second born.

Angel   It's important that you see, there are things I need /
there are things –

1st Twin   Once spoilt always spoilt –

Angel   In that house, where misery lodged / in the
neighbouring room –

1st Twin   An accident, is it wrong, son, to admit she was
  an accident –
my own / blood

Angel   I'm owed, I'm here to collect / what is owed to me –

1st Twin   You were my first born, you were the first
  I brought into this world,
you were all of / which
I wanted in a son, you were your mother's son,
the epitome of me and what I stood for,
we
were the same fabric . . . and had I of left it at that –

Angel   Duty. There is a duty, a mother and a father's duty –
there are laws and these laws keep the
world right, these laws are what keep the order of things /
   nature!
Fuckin nature, brotha, you
hear what the fuck I'm tellin' you –

1st Twin   If it had just been the two of us – son – myself
   and you,
there were places I wanted to go,
adventures we should of embarked on,
but we needed fuel, a fuel your father, Bri – never
had and so Steve / yes, Steve when he arrived, a new horizon –
an abundance of fuel –

Angel   So here I am, back to reap what was taken from me,
back for retribution –

Brotha   You've got it skewed –

1st Twin   No limits –

Angel   How? What d'you mean, skewed? –

1st Twin   No limitations to where we could go /
to what we could achieve –

Brotha   How you remembered it, your sense of things /
was blighted by Mother –

1st Twin   Never! Never again to return to that . . . the
squalor of Dunbarton Road –

Angel   Don't – no – don't put it like that – your position
in this –

Brotha   My position?

Angel   Be it left or right of centre –

Brotha   It wasn't my concern –

Angel   Your position to ignore, or better see and then fold
under the airs of your / 'creator'

Brotha   You tryina say / you insinuating –

Angel   WHY? Why would I need to insinuate / I'm offering
up – to you – a solution –

Brotha   So what, it's on me now?

Angel *attacks the circle.*

Angel   ON YOU ON HER ON HIM ON THEM!
ON ALL THOSE PARLEY BROTHA –
PARLEY TO MY OUTCAST STATE –
YOU COMMIT ROBBERY – YOU ALL COMMIT
   ROBBERY ON ME!
You all offer me up as the black sheep for
your ridicule – to justify your lies –
to solidify your gluttony – stand –

Brotha *makes to leave.*

Angel   I say where you goin?
You think you can just walk away some fifteen years later
like you did before

Brotha   Sister –

Angel   That's right –

Brotha   Ange–

Angel   Where you standing? I say where you standing on this?
You think it happened? Or you
don't think it happened?

Brotha   I'm sayin' it's easy for you – to stand there like that –
to assume the righteous position – I saw –

Angel   What? You tell me what you saw –

Brotha   None a' that which you speak –

Angel   OK – OK then, so what? You tell me what your
vigilance caught?

Brotha   You had a gripe –

Angel   Who – so what you sayin' / I?

Brotha   I'm sayin' you had a gripe with him – you had
  a gripe with Steve –
you had a gripe with
Mother – you had a gripe with me – you were gripe in general /
GRIPE!

Angel   There were reasons, or don't you recall?

Brotha   I couldn't wake up for your griping, I couldn't
  sit down
for your trying to get their
attention –

Angel   I needed to be heard –

Brotha   Exactly –

Angel   That doesn't make me . . . so what –

Brotha   Cast your mind back –

Angel   You tellin' me to cast –

Brotha   You don't remember –

Angel   What exactly?

Brotha   Your eyes on him.

Angel   I had eyes on him –

Brotha   Your eyes were set on him – you targeted him –

Angel   TO HOLY FUCK GOD GIVE ME STRENGTH
  TO DEAL WITH THIS FLIMSY CARCASS!

Brotha   That's right!

Angel   My eyes were watchful – my gaze was on him, I had
my reasons –
if you tryina to – if you
making out like I / drew him –

Brotha   Nah nah, sis – I ain't sayin' you drew his attention
I'm sayin' your aim was locked on him –
your vendetta was against him, you wanted rid of him,
for whatever reasons – you had, you
took aim, and when the time came you pulled the trigger –

Angel   When the time was right I outed him, yes –

Brotha   There's no –

Angel   At what cost? At what cost?
For you to believe?

Brotha   I believe . . .

Angel   What exactly?

Brotha   I mean, look –

Angel   If there was something I needed to tell you.
If there was something that meant I had to call
on you, if there was something so deep (*going on*)
that it might even scold your ears and
skew every audible sound – thereafter, would you listen . . . ?

Brotha   Would I?

Angel   A suttin' going on that concerned the survival of our
family . . .

You're no different from me – you're as shaped by her as I am –

Brotha   I know who the fuck / I am!

Angel   And that's it, 'bro', your damage prohibited you,
   from standing up,
like the man – you fuckin'
profess – with your ches' puffed out to be –
ah – man – all bluster – all bluster with you – all hot-headed
   pride –

Brotha   I got love, whatever you say I got love for you,
but you actin' up – I ain't standing by you –
by / it –

Angel   And even now . . . even after she reconfigure the
    family set-up –
changed the settings – and
remove our faces from the living-room frames
even now – I see it – even now – she has
control over you – even now – I see you sedated by her spell –
and now – in the present, when
I call on you to admit – to – hold yourself accountable –
to let a stranger yes – a strange white
man into the intimacies of our family – a monster – who fuckin'
beguiled you with his wallet – a
money-lending miser – to blinker your view –

There have been ample opportunities for you to step up –
and that don't mean hiding behind
your own family – that means settling debts –
that means – well you know what the fuck that
means –

Brotha   I don't have anything to say to you . . . sis . . .

Angel   Yeah, yeah, OK, stay like that – stay like that, bro –
It's all you could ever do – stay . . . just like
your father . . . what a wockless joke – you and him both –

Brotha   If you have something clear to say, then say it . . .
If you gonna stand there and just slander, then please . . .
please – tell it to someone who
actually gives a fuck –

Angel   Clear?

Brotha   Yes please.

Angel   . . . It
He – one sec –
when I'm on the (*side*)
in the – was it?

Wait . . .
(*Wait*) the memories startin' to −
when I'm in the −
upstairs − I mean downstairs (*bedroom*)
I −
whilst −
one sec
one . . .

She disarms herself.

Couzin   So that's your position?

Angel   Sec . . .

Brotha   Aha . . .

Angel   . . .

Couzin   I think you'll see that's my position also . . .

Brotha   Good. Conversation / done.

He makes to leave the stage but is stopped by **Couzin**'s *voice.*

Couzin   I saw 1st Twin recently −
With her two white children. They've grown too − they're all big!
And strong! With that pedigree look! Especially the boy −
her brand new boy − Sebastian.
He reminds me of you − green eyes − red hair − like you −
the spitting image of the twins − even
freckles − but not too much.

He has that swagger − a real swagger about him − confidence −
the kind I retain in myself −
the get-up-and-go-get-it kinda confidence − and −
we broke bread, we laughed, swapped anecdotes,
it was like old times, before all the
madness went down . . .
when we were a (*family*)
but then after they left − Sebas' and Mary −

I caught 2nd Twin in the
garden – she seemed nauseous –
so I sat with her for a bit – and asked what it was . . .
making her sick – she replied –

2nd Twin   1st Twin keeps denying her black children.
People ask – they say –
Is it just Sebastian and Mary?

1st Twin   It's just Sebas' and Mary – my two – yes –
    and Steve –
their father – my husband – that's my lot –
they're my herd . . .
they look amazing with the new house
a semi-detached
but in the city.

Couzin   So let me just leave that with you, Brotha . . .
    Peter denied Jesus –
was it 'three times'?
If she's denying your actual existence . . .
who knows what she's already denied . . . and
what . . . and who . . . three times.

Brotha *exits the stage.*

Aunty J   I know . . . What you here for . . .

Angel   Yes?

Aunty J   I know what you've come for,
but I'm afraid that thing you came for.
Well it already left
A long time ago.

Angel   Is that right?

Aunty J   What you've come for left this house a long time ago.
The blood of life
We haven't parleyed with it since

I was trying to retrieve it for you as
I heard you would be coming round . . .
Let me smoke in peace.
We tried our best, Ange . . . we – but like I say –

Angel I'm not here for your dirty money –

Aunty J Dirty? Is it now?

Angel You can't buy loyalty, surely you must of realised
 by now –

Aunty J You can rent it though, you can lease it – out . . .
It's just me and the sky line 's all I need –

Angel I ain't here for your money's. I just needed to look
 you in the eye,
one last time – and now I
see your waif-like face –
I see that there's nothing of worth for me to find here –
I see that you ain't up to the challenge . . .
I see that your campaign's over . . . Shame. I was quite
looking forward to our showdown.
But with him inside indefinitely
I see that you are alone.
Entirely alone.

Aunty J The skyline's enough –

Angel And that's enough for me . . . that price will serve
 on your head,
for playing at being spectator
when I needed you most.

For brandishing your wealth . . . thinking that your pennies
were substantial.

Aunty J That's all I've ever needed.

Angel Kept.

Aunty J Like the Incas, Angel, you know who worshipped
 the sun.

Angel   Kept, in here, kept –

Aunty J   I'm sorry I overlooked you.

Angel   In your Portobello living-room cell – kept.
In your tower of ambivalence – kept.

Aunty J   The boys are always favoured in a matriarchal set-up.

Angel   Repaid.

Settled.

Angel   That's that. I'll lay flowers at your / funeral.

Steve   You ever learn about slavery, Ange? You know slavery?
The transatlantic slave trade. At school? They ever take you
    through it?
Yeah, probably not, or if they did,
they'd give you some watered-down version of it, like a
cordial with too much tap water in, too much H_2O.

What they don't tell you is that most of the wealth
inherited in this country was due to
slavery. When you walk around areas
like Chelsea and Kensington, you look at the houses
and get to wondering
how the fuck anybody could afford to live there now . . .
but the reality is –
that money's old –
and old money was attained at the expense of others,
when it was – let's say – the done thing – to dehumanise a race
in exchange for profit . . . for free labour . . .

What they also don't teach you is that the blacks
unlike any other race, have this trait, this
'stretching back centuries tribal trait' where you seek to
'out do and enslave your neighboor'
in wartime, if there was a dispute, and one tribe won over
    the other,
they would take the fathers and make them slaves –
but not the kids – the kids got to carry on – as

they were – but the dads had to perform – a kind of
native community service –
but this slavery at least retained a kind of dignity –
it wasn't like the other slavery I was telling you
before – it didn't involve the brainwashing and subjugation
   of a race . . .

It didn't involve getting them young, you know young –
that way, if a boy is sold into slavery – if he is raised a slave –
if the family unit around him is dismantled – then what
reference does that boy have – for being an actual human?
From where does he derive his compass point?

But I breached it – slavery – the topic, 'cause I wondered
if you'd ever come across the
terminology – 'field nigger' and/or 'house nigger'?

Have you ever come across that terminology before?

No? Well it's interesting 'cause the field niggers,
were the darker slaves, the blacker ones
with harsher features, they were landed with the hardest labour,
they were – rebellious in
nature – and it was often the field niggers – or negroes –
that would burn down the big house,
plot their escape for salvation – they were deemed
the lowest of the low – and received the
hardest treatment from the master . . . but the house niggers –

Well . . . they lived in the big house, you know, a bit like ours –
the big house – as opposed to
Dunbarton Road – which we'll call the little house –
and the house negroes were normally the
offspring of field negroes who had been 'raped' by the master –
and in doing so – produced
'mixed raced children'.
High yella – low yella – golden – bronze –
they were the best of both races. Like you.
Like you
Angel.

With loose long hair like you, subtle features like you –
but still retained a sort of exoticism.
They were superior, in every way, like you . . .
but they had to serve in the big house. There
was no field behaviour from the house niggas . . . they obeyed,
    Angel, OK?

The house niggas obeyed.

Angel *goes to the tea area and brings* **Steve** *a drink.*

———————————

From outside the circle **Brian** *approaches* **1st Twin**.

Brian   She sent me round.

1st Twin   I've got nothing at all to say to you.

Brian   They sent me round –

1st Twin   They?

Brian   Your piknies – themm yes 'them'.

1st Twin   Like I said –

Brian   This about me?

1st Twin   Oh please!

Brian   Look –

1st Twin   There ain't nuttin to see but a waste a' time
    and space

Brian   Regardless of what I done to yer
back then
regardless of that –

1st Twin   Listen to you –

Brian   I'm trying. I don't need to be here

1st Twin   So why you here?

Brian   I see, I see which way you steering this –

1st Twin   Precisely –

Brian   Happy?

1st Twin   Overjoyed.

Brian   Yeah?

1st Twin   Well, thanks for popping by.

Brian   Don't think you can sweep this under the carpet.

1st Twin   She's –

Brian   A' mine and yours to do right by –

1st Twin   Right?

Brian   Exactly! Exactly, 1st Twin! So please would
    you explain
what the fuck is going on, coz what I'm
hearing – what I'm hearing, babe, it isn't good.
And suttin sharp about to kick off in here – right
now – you feel me?!

1st Twin   Just fantasies.

Beat.

1st Twin   What's been said?

Brian   Coz I ain't come through on much,
but if I got one last chance to salvage the wreckage
I'ma act concisely – you feel me, 1st Twin?
You feel me?

1st Twin   . . . You look haggard.

Brian   I tried.

He exits the stage.

Aunty J (*as Nanny*)   If it wasn't for my children, my
    ungrateful little children –
well, it's hard for you to understand,
but back then this was a rotten racist country –
and imagine poor me – with three
mixed-raced children – two of them identical with Afros out
    to here!
They were beautiful,
your mother and sister were beautiful.
Well, you can imagine – the stress – the attacks we all came
    under.
There's a bile, grandson, in many hearts, a kinda hatred
    which –
you wouldn't think was human – but it is . . .
and once you can accept that, you'll never be surprised
by anything.

They'll never – ever – ever be able to catch you off-guard.
We were special . . . we were always unique in our
eccentricities, but like I said things were
different back then, so don't waste it / don't waste you.

_____

2nd Twin   I can't say I remember much, son . . .
    of what happened.
Other than . . .
Other than . . .
Walking to school in . . .

Couzin   Walking to school in?

2nd Twin   In . . . you going out like that?

Couzin   Walking to school in what, Mum? /
Walking to school in what?!

2nd Twin   Biscuits. She used to feed us biscuits.
Most of the time.
Never, promise me you'll never bring shame on me

when you're out there – doing what you do
never walk out of the house in holey socks and always brush
   your teeth
coz a smelly breath
they won't tell you
most people won't tell you, when you're stinking
you'll just be stinking in their presence
and they'll just look at you – with that kinda glazed expression
all the while your gasses and fluids be pissin' everybody off.
Be wary of those who smile when you stink –
they're the ones
most likely to be betray you.

Enough of that, just do me proud, you've done me proud,
you always did me proud –
Just don't take cups into your room
or walk back in from the garden
without brushing off yer feet.

Squalor . . . all I remember is squalor and Nanny dancing
   naked
in the street.
Just that, an' nuttin more.

1st Twin   You were the stronger –

2nd Twin   Yes.

1st Twin   You were the rock, out of the two of us – you

2nd Twin   Hardship made me strong –
hard shit made me strong.
A fuckin'
sped-up week intensive
of all the sick twisted shit you'll ever encounter in life –

1st Twin   I'm glad I had you, I'm glad I'm of you

2nd Twin   It's supposed to be the other way round.
It's your childhood you're meant to look back on –
that time of Play-Doh dinners and fairy tales
but when I look back –

1st Twin   I never look back –

2nd Twin   When I do
on the rare occasion.

1st Twin   What's to look back on?

Beat.

I can't believe we made it out –

2nd Twin   That night? It was her or me.

1st Twin   We'd reached our limit –

2nd Twin   Exceeded our limit, you mean –

1st Twin   Well –

2nd Twin   So when I did grab her by the hair –

1st Twin   I've never seen you like that!

2nd Twin   She did feel the full effect of my rage I'd
been storing

1st Twin   And when you said –

2nd Twin   Are you coming or staying? Are you coming or
staying, sis?

1st Twin   I took my bag –

2nd Twin   Not like we had anything to pack –

1st Twin   I forgot my shoes, in a panic and just left,
with her on the floor – Mummy
in a pool of stinking piss and Golden Brew –

2nd Twin   And blood –

1st Twin   Was there?

2nd Twin   You forget already?

1st Twin   It was dark in that room –

2nd Twin   Our room, what she shared.

Aunty J (*as Nanny*)   For thine is the power and the glory . . .

2nd Twin   She'd fund her drinking campaigns with
   our child support –
I mean –
Is there no end to the woman's lawless nature?!

1st Twin   Them little red slips with our names on –
them little red slips were meant to be for us

School.

2nd Twin   Don't even talk about school.

1st Twin   On top of being mixed-race.

2nd Twin   Or half-breed mongrel I recall.

1st Twin   The whites –

2nd Twin   And the blacks, but especially the black girls,
   on us!
On us! For the fineries of our hair –

1st Twin   For the greenness of our eyes –

2nd Twin   Hated by both
but especially the black girls.

Aunty J (*as Nanny*)   A – amen.

Aunty L   She's coming round –

Aunty J   Good.

Aunty L   She's coming round later.

Aunty J   Well?

Aunty L   She'll be here soon with all her (*stuff*).

Aunty J   What time exactly?

Aunty L   Sooner, rather than later.

Aunty J   You must be relieved?

Aunty L   I think it's for the best.

Aunty J   Should a bin done a long time ago.

Aunty L   I won't let it happen again, J!

Aunty J   What?

Aunty L   I wont let it go down – like how it did before.

Aunty J   To (*you*).

Aunty L   Believe me! I can't stomach the idea.

Aunty J   I don't know what you're getting at?

Aunty L   You telling me you don't believe?

Aunty J   What exactly? Am I s'posed to believe?!

Aunty L   I always had a feeling . . . around him –

Aunty J   You know I can't / look I won't stand firm till
I have all the facts!

Aunty L   Typical!

Aunty J   No, sis / no, sis

Aunty L   She's a child!

1st Twin   I can't quite shed the remnants of shame

Aunty J   And butter wouldn't melt?

1st Twin   Of her sending me hungry to school
In odd socks.

Aunty L   Don't be flippant!

Aunty J   Just wait! JUST WAIT AND SEE. SIS!

Aunty L   If she had been mine to begin with
none a dis fuckery woulda touch!

2nd Twin   You had socks.

1st Twin   What?

2nd Twin   Yours were matching.

1st Twin   Nah, sis!

2nd Twin   It were mine that had holes in from bottom
to top.

1st Twin   And when the social services popped around
we'd –

2nd Twin   Clean up the house – we'd clean up the house.

1st Twin   Get sweets for the first time ever – she'd do our
hair –

2nd Twin   She never knew what to do with our hair!

1st Twin   Oil up our skin
Brush our teeth
Put the music on – then

2nd Twin   Invite them in, to our seemingly perfect
family –
all the while knowing –

1st Twin   It's coming back –

2nd Twin   All the while wanting to scream –

1st Twin   I can see it – I've got the image in my mind!

2nd Twin   Bitch
Bitch
Bitch I'ma kill you
For robbing me a' mine.

_____

Angel   Thanks for letting me stay here for a while.

Aunty L   There's always a place for you here, my sweetheart.

Angel   Thanks. Thanks. I appreciate it, Aunty, I really do.

Aunty L   You don't have to thank me. There's a place for
you here,
there's always been a place for you here.

Angel   There has, hasn't there? Funny innit – when you look
at it.

Aunty L   What?

Angel   How these things come to . . . (*pass*).
So where should I put my bag?

Aunty L   You listen to me, Angel, and you listen to me hard
yeah?
I got you back – I believe you, up
here we believe you.
Stand by what you say
So don't forget that, OK?
Isn't that right, Jay?
Jay?!

Aunty J   Yes.

Aunty L   Regardless of your mother, she made her choice,
that choice was made long ago
what she wanted from life, aspired to,
before you were born and nothing
nada
was ever gonna outweigh that.

Aunty J   OK, L, let the girl / put her bags (*down*).

Aunty L   It ain't that she hasn't got love in her heart
she has
and probably still even for you
but what she's gained
what she's acquired through him
means way more to her than –

Aunty J   You want / some water

Aunty L   – and that's, well, that's just the fucked-up nature
of life sometimes
It's hard
but you're loved
don't forget that by me.

Angel   Thanks . . .

Aunty L   She'll see sense –
Just remember I've sat where you sit right now
I've been that child in need
but the difference is,
daughter,
I had no one to reach out to.
That's not this situation
this situation is different
It's different, understand?
Different.

Angel   Yes, Aunty.

Aunty L   But nuttin can excuse what was done to you
and nuttin will rest till its been paid back in full.
Trust me, trust me
don't think for a second this thing won't come back around
on him
OK?

Aunty J   I think she gets / the point, L

Aunty L   But enough of that now, you look tired.
My beautiful niece here looks tired. Go rest your
head in the bedroom and I'll bring you a warm brew.

Angel   Thanks, Aunty, thanks.

1st Twin   It's on the line. Everything we have is on the line
now!

———————————————

Aunty L   I let her down –

1st Twin   Everything we've built.

Aunty J   Did you fuck?

Steve   We?

Aunty L   I let her go –

Aunty J   You –

Aunty L   After the promises I made, let 'er slip –

Aunty J   She was – it ain't as easy as . . .

Aunty L   See, you ain't got the lie to hand.

Aunty J   No –

Aunty L   And neither have I?

1st Twin   Let's go.

Steve   Where?

1st Twin   Let's go and get her – 'we' need to get her –
   before (*she*) –

Steve   Sure. Sure. I'll wait in the car.

He leaves.

Aunty L   To cover what be glaringly true –

Aunty J   Just breathe.

Aunty L   A ten-year-old in my care
depending on me
counting on me
banking on her aunty, on the vow she made to protect her
from all of what I been through before
from the wolves at the door
but when the moment finally came –

Aunty J   She got in your head, like she does, like Mother.

Aunty L   How I didn't –

Aunty J   You always did –

Aunty L   But – that's not what I'm – Will you let me finish my point?

Aunty J   Since we were (*little*) – Sorry, carry / on

Aunty L   Can I?

Aunty J   Yes / I'm just –

Aunty L   Please!

Aunty J   Yes! Yes!

Aunty L   But
when it came
when the moment finally came
and I'd bathed her
combed through her hair
her beautiful dark coolie hair –

Aunty J   Her hair was always lovely –

Aunty L   And we laughed, but actually laughed, sis,
for the first time
without the backdrop of sadness.
A complete moment of happiness achieved
and that would of been enough –
Coz we'd of had that
as a foundation
to build on but –
the bell ring – the bell rang.

Aunty J   You didn't know? She was coming up?

Aunty L   I must of forgot, coz the social services were due to make a visit,
and the court case woulda
been –

Angel   That's not how it happened!

Aunty L   Let me tell it –

Angel   Wasn't I intercepted from / school?
By 1st Twin?
Wasn't I?

Aunty L   But the bell rang, and she still in the bath, like
   an angel
the angel that she was
and so I went to the door
I opened the door –
the wolves were at the door
the two of them identical,
identical in their cause
to rescue what was rightfully theirs by (*birth*)
so you see, sis, that's why!
That's why I had to open the door!
And once they were in –

Aunty J   Calm down, sis –

Aunty L   The war had practically been lost
coz the reality is
the reality was
all she's ever craved
all she's ever wanted was the love of that woman who
conceived her – so
and her there – in the towel
already out of the bath!

1st Twin   I'll take it from here.

Aunty L   She says and I froze. I instead / of –

1st Twin   You want mummy to dry your hair? Ha? Like
   she used to?

Aunty L   Froze! Because no matter what she was
I should of stood firm!
I should of stood rooted!
But the reality is she isn't mine
Would of never be truly mine!
And I felt embarrassed, Jay – I felt like a fraud!

1st Twin   Now Mummy wants to ask you a question.

Aunty L   Coz, I knew I'd never have
what was truly between them
despite the fact of my protecting!

1st Twin   And I want you to answer. With all your honesty.
Thinking about our family. And how
much your mummy loves and cares about you.
Thinking about your brother, thinking
about yourself, and those yet to come.
And the chance to let go of what's been brainwashing us
an' embrace freedom.
Daughter –
I want you to be all you can be – I want you to be – all you
    can be!
I want you to come home and start again
how it should be done
should of been done
as a family
because that's what we are – isn't it? And what do families do?
They stand by one another – through thick and thin –
they protect each other and forgive!
I'm willing to forgive you, daughter, if you're willing to
    forgive us?
For overlooking you – for not nurturing you how we should of
with all your talent
with all your potential
But –

Aunty L   Angel! Don't listen to your mu –

1st Twin   Mother and daughter.
Mother and daughter again – the two of / us
One.

Aunty L   What?! Ange! Don't listen to your mother!

1st Twin   Is here. I'm here / aren't I?

Aunty L   PLEASE! SIS. DON'T DO IT!

1st Twin   So I want you to tell the / truth.

Aunty L   NO!

1st Twin   I want you to stop this / game.

Aunty L   ANGEL! ANGE!

1st Twin   So you can come back.

Aunty L   Right! / That's it! GET OUT! OUT!

2nd Twin   Calm down, L.

Aunty L   Calm (*down*).

1st Twin   Home.

Aunty L   ANGE? This is . . . (*home*).

Angel   . . . Home?

1st Twin   Did it happen? Did it happen? Did it? Happen? Ange? Happen?

Sharp silence.

Angel   . . . No . . . it didn't happen.

The circle starts to deconstruct.
Aunty J *and* **Steve** *leave.*

––––––––––––––––––––––––––––––––

Angel *finds herself dismantled by the memory.*

Angel   You . . .
you took me back?

Beat.

You . . .
took me back, after you'd

dried your
saved up

Skin
I lived
under the roof
same
under the same roof
As you and Steve.

Things
back went

went back to as they were
until one day
you just
rid of
got

1st Twin   I . . . ?

Angel   Rid of –

1st Twin   We –

Angel   Clean erased me.

1st Twin   I think it's time you went and lived with your grandad.

Angel   After all a that . . .
After all a (*that*)
Just
Shafted off.
Stamped
Unpackaged
Unrecorded delivery

Second-born daughter
Ange –
Goin' cheap . . .

The future. **Aunty L** *leaves.*

Angel Mum . . .

2nd Twin It's Aunty –

Angel Mum?

2nd Twin It's 2nd Twin . . .

Angel Yes . . . Aunty . . . oh, for a moment then, from
behind . . .
I thought I was staring at her . . .

2nd Twin Well, we are identical.

Angel You've always been identical, yeah, but I never
usually mix you up.

2nd Twin When you rang I was surprised. To hear
from you.

Angel I wanted to say hi – you know, pop round.

2nd Twin You should.

Angel I always loved your house –

2nd Twin We don't own it –

Angel Still always loved it. 'Cause I was living here . . . for
a bit . . . wasn't I?

2nd Twin I don't recall.

Angel Yes I was, living here for a while – when 1st Twin
was struggling –
I remember we –
you, me and Couzin – eating breakfast –
we were eating breakfast –
after I returned home . . . after it
happened –

2nd Twin We were always in range, me and your mum,
in case either us needed the help –

Angel   After it happened.

2nd Twin   It?

Angel   Yes. It.

Beat.

2nd Twin   Well, look –

Angel   I was thinking, that I'll get into music –
maybe try and get into music – a new career shift –

2nd Twin   Good for you Ange, good for you.

Beat.

Angel   Would you back me? If I went into it.

2nd Twin   Back?

Angel   Yes back, like you did Couzin.
Your son.

2nd Twin   . . . The thing is – well what with my
   grandson now –
and work – you see with my centre,
which is really taking off, I'm so proud of myself,
to think – now I have a PhD . . . to think
now – I have a practice of my own . . . where I see patients –
who are in need – of emotional reconstruction.

Beat.

2nd Twin   So . . . it's not that I won't back you . . . it's
   just that
with the commitments et cetera – I'm not sure how
available I'll be, and what with your mother –

Angel   Her.

2nd Twin   Yes, she . . . well –

Angel   I understand.

Silence.

2nd Twin   Have you seen Couzin recently?

Angel   Yes. We spoke last week.

2nd Twin   Living in Hampstead now, Hampstead, can you believe that?

Angel   Hampstead?

2nd Twin   Yes, a home-owner in Hampstead. Have you ever been up there?

Angel   I've never been to Hampstead, no.

2nd Twin   Where the elite have their quarters – the elite –
my son – who would of thought, aye?
Elite.

Angel   I would of thought.

2nd Twin   Yeah?

Angel   He had you after all, didn't he?

2nd Twin   Yes . . . that's what I keep on saying.

Beat.

Angel   You would of taken me, wouldn't you?
You would of taken me on?
I would of inherited you – wouldn't I?
If your ties weren't so wedded to 1st Twin – my (*mother*).
After all you shared a womb.
you're identical.
I can't hold that against you, can I?
Can I?
You're more or less the same person
'cept you never traded off your (*offspring*).
Strangely
out of everyone
it's you who I forgive,
forgive for not acting in the proper way –
there are some ties, aren't there?
That go beyond truth,
go beyond what's right and just

Like the ties of mother and daughter
And yet both of us have never encountered that.

2nd Twin   No . . .

She leaves the circle. Only **Angel**, **Couzin** *and* **1st Twin** *remain.*

———————————————

Couzin *takes up the strongest position in the fragmented circle.*

Couzin   You're here . . . having lost. And now you need something from me.

1st Twin   Yes.

Couzin   You find yourself in a position of need.

1st Twin   I am in need yes, need, nephew.

Couzin   Have you seen your daughter recently?

Beat.

1st Twin   So if you can / help –

Couzin   Dropped in to see your grandchildren.

1st Twin   Or if this is a bad time –

Couzin   You have four I do believe.

1st Twin   There hasn't been time.

Couzin   You never quite graduated to grandmother, did you?

Still reeling from the role of mother.

1st Twin   If you can't help just / say –

Couzin   Most mothers when they get old are invigorated by their grandchildren's energy –

1st Twin   I'm losing the house – I stand to lose the house, without your help –
Steve's / gone

Couzin   A new lease of life, it triggers a nostalgia 'they say'
and in some way, the grandmother and
the grandchild meet in the middle of wisdom and innocence –
and in that union both are –
reinvented.

1st Twin   There are reasons I no longer see my daughter,
reasons you wouldn't begin to understand –

Couzin   But now your here wanting my help
and all I can see are the people – 'you'
'abandoned' all I can hear are their whys? –

1st Twin   When you have your own, you'll understand –

Couzin   I'll help you, 1st Twin . . . but first you're gonna
have to say it.

1st Twin   Thank you . . . thank you so much, nephew,
you've done so well, it's incredible how well
you've done – it is really – you've taken the family name
to unbelievable heights, and you're a
good soul, you've never forgotten where you came from,
your mother – my sister – 2nd Twin installed,
that in you as we installed it in each other –
when we made a choice to live – and not just to survive –

Couzin   And when you've said it . . . then you can have
    the money,
but you have to admit it . . . and I
have to see you admit it. That's all, nothing more.

1st Twin   What do I need to admit?

Couzin   You know, exactly what I'm getting at. You have
    to admit.
That you knew . . . and yet still – put
your own mortality first – you have to admit –
that despite knowing – there was a part of you –
that was able – to ignore –
you have to admit, that despite knowing
you carried on laying next to the monster who

inflicted lasting pain, on your first-born daughter –
you have to admit, that he coerced you into –
trading off your two black children,
you have to admit –
you deny those children as your own
when engaged in what you call 'civilised conversation'
you have to admit – that you had it in you
and you have to mean it when you say it.

Well . . .

1st Twin   I know none of that which you speak –

Couzin   There it is then –

He makes to leaves.

1st Twin   Wait. Wait. Wait, Couzin.

Couzin   Are you ready to say it?

1st Twin   I'm sorry –

Couzin   This isn't about apologies . . .

1st Twin   She said it never happened!
That's what she said.

Couzin   She was ten . . . she (*was*)
Fuck this

He makes to leave.

1st Twin   I admit to . . .

Couzin   Did you know?

1st Twin   I –

Couzin   Did you know?

1st Twin   We –

Couzin   Did you know? About Steve and Angel?

1st Twin   I . . . had my suspicions –

Couzin   Did you know?!

1st Twin   . . . I –

Couzin   I'm gone –

1st Twin   I . . . knew –

Couzin   What?

1st Twin   – something was up.

Couzin   And yet you made her retract her story?

1st Twin   Yes . . . I mean, kind of –

Couzin   What?

1st Twin   Yes . . . it was the best solution for everyone
involved . . . We –

We, couldn't return to Dunbarton –

We –

Couzin   You –

1st Twin   I . . . couldn't return to Dunbarton Road . . .

Couzin   There it is then.

1st Twin   So will you give me the money?

Couzin   . . . Balance transfer or a cheque?

1st Twin *leaves. Only* **Angel** *and* **Couzin** *remain.*

———————————

Couzin   Yes cozy wa gwan?

Angel   Oh you know –

Couzin   No I don't – pray tell sista! Pray (*tell*).

Angel   Sister now, is it?

Couzin   No?

Angel   Of course, sis!

Couzin   That's right.

Beat.

Angel   Do you . . .

Couzin   What?

Angel   Do you ever see her?

Couzin   Your mother?

Angel   Yeah, do you have any contact with her –

Couzin   No, only when she visits Mum –

Angel   Which is often?

Couzin   Yeah . . . often enough. You know the twins – thick as thieves.

Angel   How does she seem?

Couzin   Different –

Angel   How does she look?

Couzin   Older . . .

Angel   Older than 2nd Twin?

Couzin   They've aged differently.

Angel   Yeah?

Couzin   Your mother has life's burden on her face.

Angel   Well, thass no surprise!

Couzin   Always bewilders me – how two women can have exactly the same genetic make-up and yet . . .

Angel   Go on.

Couzin   One withers more quickly then the other –

Angel   What you are eventually shows in yer face –

Couzin   Who said that?

Angel   I did –

Couzin   So you did –

Angel   No, but really –

Couzin   I know –

Angel   And yet still, Couzin, and yet still! After all of that, after all of fucking that – I still miss her.

I still – does she ask after me?

Nah. She's got new pikinies now anyways.
My religion says I have to honour my father and my mother.

Couzin   That's good –

Angel   So I'm trying my best –

Couzin   Yeah.

Angel   But it ain't easy

Couzin   No.

Angel   When they both wockless people.

Beat.

Is she still with him?

Couzin   I think . . .

Angel   She still lays next to him?

Couzin   Aha –

Angel   What a woman –

Couzin   Well –

Angel   What a (*woman*), there really are no limits to this degradation –

Couzin   Her skin –

Angel   Yeah?

Couzin   When she lays next to him.
Crawls apparently so −

Angel   She knows − she's always known − but . . . what was
    done to me −
how a child could get vilified
like that − coerced and manipulated into
saying it never / happened

Couzin   Please − we both know, yeah, and I'm not saying
you don't have a right to grieve but just,
please − please let this go −

Angel   What?

Couzin   Not for them, not for him . . . but, for you, Ange,
otherwise I'm fearful −

Angel   The debt is hers.

Couzin   I'm fearful that you'll forever be transfixed to that
    spot −
to that space in time / to that −

Angel   They need to know − my sister needs to know −

Couzin   Half-sister and from him who you now seek to
destroy.

Angel   They need to know what they're living with −
They need to know, what he's capable of −

Couzin   Or I fear, Ange − I fear that soon, your face will
    reflect your burden −

Angel   Don't watch my face − you think I care about my face?

Couzin   This ain't your cross to bear −

Angel   It's not? It's − then who's fucking cross is this to bear!

Couzin   We've all bore it −

Angel   No!

Couzin   We all bear it now!

Angel   OK –

Couzin   We all bear it for failing an eight-year-old child . . .
There was a chance for this family, but when
the time came to act accordingly / and restore a long missing
   integrity –

Angel   Please tell me where you going with this, Couzin?!

Couzin   It imploded! It couldn't stand up – it never had the
   legs to!

Look – look at the wreckage! There is no us! There's no family!
There's just memories . . .
And even they are questionable – even they've become
   tarnished – by –

Angel   This is not on me –

Couzin   Nobody's saying that –

Angel   She had me retract my statement – in exchange for –
She had me deny my truth – she –
did what she could to maintain the luxury –

Couzin   She could never return to Dunbarton Road!

Angel   The Lexus saloons and Luis Vuitton bags – the –

Couzin   She had her demons – the – the squalor of the
   past, it –

Angel   I've forgone my integrity, Couzin!
I've forgone my integrity, Cozzy! I've forgone my
truth – it's gone – I . . . and this is why I'm back –

Couzin   This isn't your battle –

Angel   This is why I'm here!

Angel   I'm here to reclaim my truth –

Couzin   You have your truth –

Angel   I'm bigger now –

Couzin   OK –

Angel   I'm big and I'm back to regain my truth

Couzin   Not like this –

Angel   I'm no different, am I?

Couzin   Where you going with this?

Angel   I'm no different. I'm no different from her –
I'm my mother's daughter! I'm my
mother's daughter, Cozzy . . . I'm –

Couzin   You have your faith –

Angel   She . . . this is her victory –

Couzin   No –

Angel   She . . . really never asks after me?

Couzin   . . .

Silence.

Black.

End of play.